fresh and healthy
vegetarian

over 150 tempting vegetarian dishes for all tastes and every occasion

valerie ferguson

This edition is published by Southwater

Southwater is an imprint of Anness Publishing Ltd
Hermes House, 88–89 Blackfriars Road, London SE1 8HA
tel. 020 7401 2077; fax 020 7633 9499
www.southwaterbooks.com; info@anness.com

© Anness Publishing Ltd 2003

This edition distributed in the UK by The Manning Partnership
Ltd, 6 The Old Dairy, Melcombe Road, Bath BA2 3LR;
tel. 01225 478 444; fax 01225 478 440;
sales@manning-partnership.co.uk

This edition distributed in the USA and Canada by
National Book Network, 4720 Boston Way, Lanham, MD
20706; tel. 301 459 3366; fax 301 459 1705;
www.nbnbooks.com

This edition distributed in Australia by Pan Macmillan Australia,
Level 18, St Martins Tower, 31 Market St, Sydney, NSW 2000;
tel. 1300 135 113; fax 1300 135 103;
customer.service@macmillan.com.au

This edition distributed in New Zealand by The Five Mile Press
(NZ) Ltd, PO Box 33–1071 Takapuna, Unit 11/101–111
Diana Drive, Glenfield, Auckland 10; tel. (09) 444 4144;
fax (09) 444 4518; fivemilenz@clear.net.nz

A CIP catalogue record for this book is available from the
British Library.

Publisher: Joanna Lorenz
Managing Editor: Helen Sudell
Editorial Reader: Linda Doeser
Production Controller: Claire Rae

Previously published as part of a larger compendium, Vegetarian

10 9 8 7 6 5 4 3 2 1

ACKNOWLEDGEMENTS

Recipes contributed by: Catherine Atkinson, Alex
Barker, Michelle Berriedale-Johnson, Angela
Boggiano, Kathy Brown, Carla Capalbo, Kit Chan,
Jacqueline Clark, Carole Clements, Trish Davies, Roz
Denny, Patrizia Diemling, Matthew Drennan, Sarah
Edmonds, Rafi Fernandez, Christine France, Silvano
Franco, Shirley Gill, Nicola Graimes, Rosamund
Grant, Carole Handslip, Rebekah Hassan, Deh-Ta
Hsuing, Shehzad Husain, Christine Ingram, Judy
Jackson, Manisha Kanani, Soheila Kimberley, Sara
Lewis, Patricia Lousada, Lesley Mackley, Sue Maggs,
Kathy Man, Sally Mansfield, Norma Miller, Sallie
Morris, Annie Nichols, Maggie Pannell, Katherine
Richmond, Jennie Shapter, Anne Sheasby, Liz Trigg,
Hilaire Walden, Laura Washburn, Steven Wheeler,
Elizabeth Wolf-Cohen, Jeni Wright.

Photography: William Adams-Lingwood, Karl
Adamson, Edward Allwright, Steve Baxter, Nicki
Dowey, James Duncan, John Freeman, Ian Garlick,
Michelle Garrett, John Heseltine, Amanda Heywood,
Ferguson Hill, Janine Hosegood, David Jordan, Dave
King, Don Last, Patrick McLeavey, Michael Michaels,
Steve Moss, Thomas Odulate, Simon Smith, Sam
Stowell, Polly Wreford.

NOTES

Bracketed terms are intended for American readers.

For all recipes, quantities are given in both metric
and imperial measures and, where appropriate,
measures are also given in standard cups and spoons.
Follow one set, but not a mixture, because they are
not interchangeable.

Medium (US large) eggs are used throughout unless
otherwise stated.

Standard spoon and cup measures are level.

1 tsp = 5ml, 1 tbsp = 15ml, 1 cup = 250ml/8fl oz.

Australian standard tablespoons are 20ml. Australian
readers should use 3 tsp in place of 1 tbsp for
measuring small quantities of flour, salt, etc.

fresh and healthy
vegetarian

Contents

Introduction

A diet based on fresh produce is almost by definition healthy. This is not just because vegetables and fruit are good sources of essential vitamins and minerals, high in fibre and low in fats. It is also because they are so versatile that it is easy to eat a varied diet, which is the

secret of healthy eating. Of course, we need more than just the daily five portions of fruit and vegetables recommended by nutritionists. Fortunately, there is an increasing range of fresh-tasting, high-quality vegetarian ingredients available, from tofu to pasta and rice and from nuts and seeds to pulses. However, choosing the right ingredients is only the first step – how you prepare and cook them is just as important. Most of us are already aware that fried food forms a huge part of the Western diet and anyone at all conscious of their own and their family's health limits their intake. However, it is equally essential to use cooking techniques that preserve, as far as possible, the nutritional content of the ingredients. This book contains more than 150 recipes that will help you do exactly that. However, just because they are healthy, doesn't mean they aren't bursting with flavour. There are dishes for all occasions and all tastes, from hot and spicy to subtle and delicate and from light and refreshing summery lunches to warming and substantial winter suppers.

The book is divided into five chapters, so it is easy to find exactly the right recipe for your particular needs. Soups, Dips, Appetizers & Breads offers a fabulous collection of mouth-watering recipes for hors d'oeuvres, snacks, party foods and light lunches. Cold and hot soups, spicy or creamy dips and refreshing salads will prove irresistible temptations, while home-made bread, crackers, scones and breadsticks are always popular treats.

Meals in Minutes is a life-saver for the busy cook and this collection of tasty stir-fries, pasta dishes, curries and vegetable medleys gives a completely new meaning to the expression fast food. In little more than the time it takes for another member of the family – you hope – to lay the table, you can rustle up an aromatic dish of Vegetable Kashmiri, an attractive platter of Tagliatelle with Pea Sauce, Asparagus & Broad Beans or a sizzling Lentil Stir-fry.

Life is not always conducted on the run, so Midweek Meals gives you the opportunity to create marvellous dishes in a slightly more leisurely fashion. Even so, many of these recipes, such as Spiced Couscous with Halloumi and Spring Vegetable Omelette, are very quick and easy. This chapter also features filling casseroles and stews that will satisfy the hungriest family, while some of the imaginative pasta and rice dishes would be perfect for informal supper parties.

When you want to push the boat out, turn to Special Occasion Dishes for a sophisticated array of dinner party and celebration main courses. Seduce your guests with melt-in-the-mouth Red Pepper & Watercress Filo Purses, beguile them with pretty Broccoli & Chestnut Terrine or dazzle them with colourful Ratatouille Pancakes.

No meal is complete without the proper accompaniments, although these are often

overlooked until the last minute. Side Dishes & Salads will inspire you to mix and match vegetables, rice, noodles, grains and salads with panache and style.

Finally, the end section of the book offers a mass of hints and tips on buying, storing and preparing common vegetarian ingredients, plus some useful basic recipes to help make sure that every dish you cook is packed with flavour and bursting with goodness.

SOUPS, DIPS, APPETIZERS & BREADS

Not only are the recipes in this chapter utterly delicious, but they are also wonderfully versatile. Elegant chilled soups make a refreshing start to a summer dinner party, while a steaming bowl of broth provides a warming and substantial snack served with a chunk of fresh bread – and there are fabulous recipes for all kinds of loaves here, too. Child or adult, everyone loves dips and they make perfect party food, unusual hors d'oeuvres, tasty treats with pre-dinner drinks, healthy after-school snacks and can also be served as part of a mezze for a light, summery meal.

For more formal occasions, there are recipes for appetizers that tempt the eye as well as the taste buds and will guarantee that the meal gets off to the right start. Making bread is almost as satisfying as eating a freshly baked loaf and these recipes are sure to impress both friends and family. Finally, while you are having a baking session, why not try your hand at the collection of savoury biscuits and crackers? Serve them with soup for a light lunch or with a choice of cheeses at the end of a meal – so much more flavoursome and attractive than anything you can buy in the supermarket.

You will find here a choice of familiar favourites, such as Hummus with Crudités, classic dishes, such as Stuffed Mushrooms, exotic recipes, such as Lemon & Coconut Dhal, and contemporary innovations, such as Fat-free Saffron Dip. You can mix and match with the main course recipes in the following chapters or follow an ethnic theme, such as Middle Eastern or Indian, throughout the meal. Whatever dish you serve, you can rest assured that it will be packed with flavour and full of goodness.

Chilled Tomato & Sweet Pepper Soup

Roasted red peppers give this chilled soup a sweet and slightly smoky flavour that is delicious with sun-ripened tomatoes.

Serves 4
2 red (bell) peppers, halved and seeded
45ml/3 tbsp olive oil
1 onion, finely chopped
2 garlic cloves, crushed
675g/1½lb ripe tomatoes
150ml/¼ pint/⅔ cup red wine
600ml/1 pint/2½ cups vegetable stock
salt and ground black pepper
chopped fresh chives, to garnish

For the croûtons
2 slices day-old white bread, crusts removed
60ml/4 tbsp olive oil

1 Place the pepper halves, skin side up, on a grill (broiler) rack and grill (broil) until the skins have charred. Transfer to a bowl and cover with crumpled kitchen paper. Leave to cool slightly.

2 Heat the oil in a large pan. Add the onion and garlic and cook until soft. Meanwhile, remove the skin from the peppers and coarsely chop them. Cut the tomatoes into chunks.

3 Add the peppers and tomatoes to the pan, then cover and cook gently for 10 minutes. Pour in the wine and cook for 5 minutes more, then add the stock. Season well and continue to simmer for 20 minutes.

4 For the croûtons, cut the bread into cubes. Heat the oil in a small frying pan, add the bread cubes and cook until golden. Drain on kitchen paper. When cold, store in an airtight box.

5 Process the soup in a blender or food processor until smooth. Pour into a clean glass or ceramic bowl and leave to cool thoroughly before chilling in the refrigerator for at least 3 hours. Serve the soup in chilled bowls, topped with the croûtons and garnished with chopped chives.

Gazpacho

Tomatoes, cucumber and peppers form the basis of this classic chilled soup.

Serves 4
2 slices day-old white bread
600ml/1 pint/2½ cups chilled water
1kg/2¼lb tomatoes
1 cucumber
1 red (bell) pepper, halved, seeded and chopped
1 fresh green chilli, seeded and chopped
2 garlic cloves, chopped
30ml/2 tbsp extra virgin olive oil
juice of 1 lime and 1 lemon
a few drops of Tabasco sauce
salt and ground black pepper
a handful of fresh basil leaves, to garnish
ice cubes and Avocado Salsa (optional), to serve

For the garlic croûtons
2 slices day-old white bread, crusts removed
1 garlic clove, halved
15ml/1 tbsp olive oil

1 Soak the bread in 150ml/¼ pint/⅔ cup of the chilled water for 5 minutes. Meanwhile, place the tomatoes in a bowl and pour over boiling water to cover. Leave for 30 seconds, then drain, peel, seed and chop the flesh.

2 Peel the cucumber thinly, then cut it in half lengthways and scoop out the seeds with a teaspoon. Discard the seeds and chop the flesh.

3 Place the soaked bread, tomatoes, cucumber, red pepper, chilli, garlic, olive oil, lime juice, lemon juice and Tabasco sauce in a food processor or blender, with the remaining chilled water. Process until thoroughly combined but still chunky. Pour the soup into a bowl, season to taste with salt and pepper and chill in the refrigerator for 2–3 hours.

4 Make the croûtons. Rub the surface of the bread slices with the cut garlic clove. Cube the bread and toss with the olive oil until evenly coated. Heat a large non-stick frying pan and cook the croûtons over a medium heat until crisp and golden. Drain on kitchen paper.

5 Ladle the soup into bowls and add two ice cubes to each portion. Garnish with the basil. Top with the avocado salsa, if using, and hand the croûtons separately.

Avocado Salsa

Serve a spoonful of this tasty salsa on top of each portion of Gazpacho, or enjoy it on its own, with French bread.

Serves 4
1 ripe avocado
5ml/1 tsp lemon juice
2.5cm/1in piece cucumber, diced
½ fresh red chilli, finely chopped

1 Cut the avocado in half, remove the stone (pit), then peel. Dice the flesh and put it in a bowl. Toss immediately with the lemon juice to prevent it from browning.

2 Mix the avocado with the diced cucumber and finely chopped chilli. Serve as soon as possible.

Cold Cucumber & Yogurt Soup with Walnuts

Walnuts make an interesting addition to this refreshing cold soup.

Serves 5–6
1 cucumber
4 garlic cloves, peeled
2.5ml/ ½ tsp salt
75g/3oz/ ¾ cup walnut pieces
40g/1½oz day-old white bread, torn into pieces
30ml/2 tbsp walnut oil

400ml/14fl oz/1⅔ cups natural (plain) yogurt
120ml/4fl oz/ ½ cup chilled still mineral water
5–10ml/1–2 tsp lemon juice

For the garnish
40g/1½oz/scant ½ cup walnuts, coarsely chopped
25ml/5 tsp olive oil
fresh dill sprigs

1 Cut the cucumber in half lengthways. Peel one half. Dice both halves, so that you have a mixture of peeled and unpeeled pieces of cucumber. Set aside.

2 Crush the garlic and salt together in a mortar with a pestle. Add the walnuts and crush them into the mixture, then work in the bread. When the mixture is smooth, gradually add the walnut oil, using the pestle to make sure that the mixture is thoroughly combined.

3 Scrape the mixture into a large bowl. Beat in the yogurt and diced cucumber, then beat in the mineral water and lemon juice to taste. Chill the soup if you have time.

4 Pour the soup into chilled soup bowls. Sprinkle the coarsely chopped walnuts on top, then drizzle a little olive oil over the nuts. Complete the garnish with the fresh dill.

Cook's Tip
If you like your soup smooth, process it in a food processor or blender to a purée before serving.

Chilled Almond Soup

Unless you want to spend a lot of time pounding the ingredients for this refreshing Spanish soup by hand, a food processor is an essential kitchen tool.

Serves 6
4 slices day-old white bread, crusts removed
750ml/1¼ pints/3 cups chilled water

115g/4oz/1 cup blanched almonds
2 garlic cloves, sliced
75ml/5 tbsp olive oil
25ml/5 tsp sherry vinegar
salt and ground black pepper
toasted flaked (sliced) almonds and skinned seedless grapes, to garnish

1 Tear the bread into a bowl and pour over 150ml/ ¼ pint/ ⅔ cup of the chilled water. Leave for 5 minutes.

2 Put the almonds and garlic in a blender or food processor and process until very finely ground. Add the soaked white bread and process until smooth.

3 With the motor running, gradually add the oil through the lid or feeder tube until the mixture forms a smooth paste. Add the sherry vinegar and remaining chilled water and process until smooth and thoroughly combined.

4 Scrape the mixture into a bowl and season with salt and pepper, adding a little more water if the soup is very thick. Chill in the refrigerator for at least 3 hours.

5 Ladle the soup into chilled bowls and sprinkle with the toasted almonds and skinned grapes.

Cook's Tip
To blanch almonds, put the kernels in a bowl, pour over boiling water and leave for about 5 minutes. Drain, then rub off the skins with the palms of your hands.

Pea, Leek & Broccoli Soup

A delicious and nutritious soup, ideal for a family supper to warm those chilly winter evenings.

Serves 4–6
1 onion, chopped
225g/8oz/2 cups sliced leeks
225g/8oz unpeeled
   potatoes, diced
900ml/1 ½ pints/3¾ cups
   vegetable stock
1 bay leaf
225g/8oz/2 cups broccoli florets
175g/6oz/1 ½ cups frozen peas
30–45ml/2–3 tbsp chopped
   fresh parsley
salt and ground black pepper
fresh parsley leaves, to garnish

1 Put the onion, leeks, potatoes, stock and bay leaf in a large, heavy pan and mix together well. Cover and bring to the boil over a medium heat. Lower the heat and simmer, stirring frequently, for 10 minutes.

2 Add the broccoli and peas, cover and return to the boil. Lower the heat and simmer, stirring occasionally, for a further 10 minutes.

3 Set aside to cool slightly. Remove and discard the bay leaf. Process the soup in a blender or food processor, in batches if necessary, until a smooth purée.

4 Add the parsley, season to taste with salt and pepper and process again briefly. Return to the pan and reheat gently until piping hot. Ladle into heated soup bowls and garnish with parsley leaves. Serve immediately.

Variations
• If you prefer, cut the vegetables finely and leave the cooked soup chunky rather than puréeing it.
• The potatoes can be peeled before cooking, but the soup will contain less fibre and fewer nutrients.
• Substitute frozen or drained, canned corn kernels for the frozen peas.

Spiced Indian Cauliflower Soup

Light and tasty, this creamy, mildly spicy soup makes a wonderfully warming first course. It would also make a delicious light lunch with some Indian bread.

Serves 4–6
1 large potato, diced
1 small cauliflower, chopped
1 onion, chopped
15ml/1 tbsp sunflower oil
45ml/3 tbsp water
1 garlic clove, crushed
15ml/1 tbsp grated fresh
   root ginger
10ml/2 tsp ground turmeric
5ml/1 tsp cumin seeds
5ml/1 tsp black mustard seeds
10ml/2 tsp ground coriander
1 litre/1¾ pints/4 cups
   vegetable stock
300ml/ ½ pint/1 ¼ cups natural
   (plain) yogurt
salt and ground black pepper
fresh coriander (cilantro) or
   parsley sprigs, to garnish

1 Put the potato, cauliflower and onion into a large, heavy pan with the oil and water. Cook over a medium heat until hot and bubbling, then cover and lower the heat. Continue cooking the mixture for about 10 minutes.

2 Add the garlic, ginger, turmeric, cumin seeds, mustard seeds and ground coriander. Stir well and cook for 2 minutes more, stirring occasionally.

3 Pour in the stock and season to taste with salt and pepper. Bring to the boil, then lower the heat, cover and simmer for about 20 minutes.

4 Stir in the yogurt and adjust the seasoning, if necessary. Ladle the soup into heated bowls, garnish with fresh coriander or parsley sprigs and serve immediately.

Variation
This soup is equally delicious chilled. After simmering, let it cool, then stir in the yogurt. Chill in the refrigerator for 4–6 hours before serving in chilled bowls.

Jerusalem Artichoke Soup

Thanks to their mild, nutty flavour, Jerusalem artichokes make a remarkably good, creamy soup.

Serves 4
30ml/2 tbsp olive oil
1 large onion, chopped
1 garlic clove, chopped
1 celery stick, chopped
675g/1½lb Jerusalem artichokes, peeled or scrubbed and chopped
1.2 litres/2 pints/5 cups vegetable stock
300ml/½ pint/1¼ cups milk
salt and ground black pepper
Gruyère Toasts, to serve (optional)

1 Heat the oil in a large pan and cook the onion, garlic and celery over a medium heat, stirring occasionally, for about 5 minutes, or until softened. Add the Jerusalem artichokes and cook for 5 minutes more.

2 Add the stock and season with salt and pepper to taste. Bring to the boil, lower the heat and simmer, stirring occasionally, for 20–25 minutes, until the artichokes are tender.

3 Transfer the soup to a food processor or blender and process until smooth. Return the soup to the pan, stir in the milk and heat through gently for 2 minutes. Ladle the soup into bowls and top with Gruyère Toasts, if using, and ground black pepper.

Gruyère Toasts

These are very good when floated on Jerusalem Artichoke Soup, but can also be served as snacks.

Makes 8
8 slices French bread
115g/4oz/1 cup grated Gruyère cheese

1 Spread out the slices of French bread in a grill (broiler) pan and toast them lightly on one side under a hot grill.
2 Turn the slices of bread over and sprinkle the untoasted side of each with the grated Gruyère. Grill (broil) until the cheese melts and is golden.

Spinach & Rice Soup

Use young spinach leaves to prepare this light and fresh-tasting soup.

Serves 4
675g/1½lb fresh young spinach, washed
45ml/3 tbsp extra virgin olive oil
1 small onion, finely chopped
2 garlic cloves, finely chopped
1 small fresh red chilli, seeded and finely chopped
200g/7oz/1 cup risotto rice
1.2 litres/2 pints/5 cups vegetable stock
salt and ground black pepper
60ml/4 tbsp grated pecorino cheese, to serve

1 Place the spinach in a large pan with just the water that clings to its leaves after washing. Add a large pinch of salt. Heat gently until the spinach has just wilted, then remove from the heat and drain, reserving any liquid.

2 Either chop the spinach finely using a large knife or place it in a food processor and process to a fairly coarse purée.

3 Heat the oil in a large, heavy pan. Add the onion, garlic and red chilli and cook over a low heat, stirring occasionally, for 4–5 minutes, until softened.

4 Add the rice and stir until all the grains are well coated, then pour in the stock and reserved spinach liquid. Bring to the boil over a medium heat, then lower the heat and simmer for about 10 minutes.

5 Add the spinach and season with salt and pepper to taste. Cook for 5–7 minutes more, until the rice is tender. Check the seasoning and serve in warmed soup plates with the grated pecorino cheese.

> **Cook's Tip**
> Use arborio or carnaroli rice for the rice soup, or try one of the less familiar risotto rices, such as Vialone Nano.

Spiced Carrot Dip

This is a delicious low-fat dip with a sweet and spicy flavour. Serve with wheat crackers or tortilla chips.

Serves 4
1 onion
4 carrots
grated rind and juice of 2 oranges
15ml/1 tbsp hot curry paste
150ml/¼ pint/⅔ cup low-fat natural (plain) yogurt
a handful of fresh basil leaves
15–30ml/1–2 tbsp fresh lemon juice, to taste
Tabasco sauce, to taste
salt and ground black pepper

1 Chop the onion finely. Peel and grate the carrots. Place three-quarters of the grated carrot in a small pan and add the onion, orange rind and juice and curry paste. Bring to the boil, lower the heat, cover and simmer for 10 minutes, until tender.

2 Allow to cool slightly, then process the mixture in a blender or food processor until smooth. Scrape into a bowl and leave to cool completely.

3 Stir in the yogurt, a little at a time. Tear the basil leaves into small pieces and stir them into the mixture.

4 Season with lemon juice, Tabasco, salt and pepper to taste. Mix well. Serve at room temperature within a few hours of making. Garnish with the remaining grated carrot.

> **Cook's Tip**
> The original Tabasco sauce, dating from the mid-nineteenth century, is made from red chillies, vinegar and salt. A green chilli version is also available.

> **Variation**
> Greek (US strained plain) yogurt or sour cream can be used instead of natural (plain) yogurt to make a richer, creamy dip.

Fat-free Saffron Dip

Serve this mild dip with fresh vegetable crudités – it is particularly good with crunchy vegetables, such as cauliflower florets, baby corn cobs and celery.

Serves 4
15ml/1 tbsp boiling water
small pinch of saffron threads
200ml/7fl oz/scant 1 cup fat-free fromage frais (farmer's cheese)
10 fresh chives
10 fresh basil leaves
salt and ground black pepper

1 Pour the boiling water into a small bowl and add the saffron threads. Leave to infuse (steep) for 3 minutes.

2 Beat the fromage frais until smooth, then stir in the infused saffron liquid.

3 Use a pair of scissors to snip the chives into the dip. Tear the basil leaves into small pieces and stir them in. Season with salt and pepper to taste and stir to combine. Serve immediately.

> **Variation**
> If you like, you can omit the saffron and flavour the dip with a squeeze of lemon or lime juice instead.

Pesto Dip

This tastes fabulous with roasted vegetables and also goes very well with baked potato skins and chips (French fries).

Serves 4
250ml/8fl oz/1 cup sour cream or low-fat fromage frais (farmer's cheese)
15ml/1 tbsp ready-made pesto

1 Spoon the sour cream or fromage frais into a bowl. Stir in the pesto, swirling it on the surface of the dip.
2 Cover and chill until ready to serve.

Bean, Watercress & Herb Dip

A refreshing dip that is especially good served with crudités and breadsticks.

Serves 4–6
225g/8oz/1 cup plain
   cottage cheese
400g/14oz can butter (lima)
   beans, drained and rinsed
1 bunch spring onions
   (scallions), chopped
50g/2oz watercress, chopped
60ml/4 tbsp mayonnaise
45ml/3 tbsp chopped fresh
   mixed herbs
salt and ground black pepper
watercress sprigs, to garnish

1 Put the cottage cheese, butter beans, spring onions, watercress, mayonnaise and herbs in a blender or food processor and process to a coarse purée.

2 Spoon the mixture into a dish, season to taste with salt and pepper and cover tightly with clear film (plastic wrap). Chill in the refrigerator for several hours.

3 Transfer to a serving dish or individual dishes and garnish with watercress sprigs. Serve with crudités and breadsticks.

Curried Corn Dip

Serve this spicy dip with crudités, breadsticks or Melba toast.

Serves 6–8
30ml/2 tbsp mayonnaise
10–15ml/2–3 tsp curry paste
225g/8oz/1 cup cottage cheese
115g/4oz/1 cup grated
   Cheddar cheese
300ml/½ pint/1¼ cups
   sour cream
115g/4oz/⅔ cup canned
   corn, drained
salt and ground black pepper

1 Blend the mayonnaise, curry paste and cottage cheese together in a bowl. Stir in the grated Cheddar.
2 Stir in the sour cream and corn and season with salt and pepper to taste. Transfer to a serving bowl and serve.

Hummus with Crudités

Always a great family favourite, hummus can be made quickly at home with the help of a blender.

Serves 2–3
400g/14oz can chickpeas
30ml/2 tbsp tahini
30ml/2 tbsp lemon juice
1 garlic clove, crushed
salt and ground black pepper
olive oil and paprika, to garnish

To serve
whole baby carrots and radishes
strips of green and red (bell)
   pepper, chicory (Belgian
   endive), celery and cucumber
bitesize chunks of bread, pitta or
   grissini sticks

1 Drain the chickpeas and put them in a blender or food processor. Add the tahini, lemon juice and garlic. Process to a smooth paste.

2 Season the hummus with plenty of salt and pepper. Spoon it into a bowl and swirl the top with the back of a spoon. Trickle over a little olive oil and sprinkle with paprika.

3 Arrange the baby carrots, radishes and the strips of salad vegetables around the rim of a large plate.

4 Add chunks of bread, pieces of pitta or grissini. Place the bowl of hummus in the centre. Serve immediately.

Variation
Hummus is delicious served with hot celeriac fritters. Peel and slice one medium celeriac into strips about 1cm/½in wide and 5cm/2in long. Drop them into a bowl of water mixed with a little lemon juice. Lightly beat one egg in a shallow dish. In another shallow dish, combine 115g/4oz/1 cup ground almonds, 45ml/3 tbsp grated Parmesan cheese and 45ml/ 3 tbsp chopped fresh parsley. Heat vegetable oil for deep-frying to 180°C/350°F or until a cube of bread browns in about 30 seconds. Pat the celeriac dry and dip, first, in the egg and then in the almond mixture. Deep-fry, in batches, and serve.

Cannellini Bean Dip

This soft bean dip or pâté is good spread on wheat crackers or toasted muffins. Serve it with wedges of tomato and salad leaves.

Serves 4
400g/14oz can cannellini beans, rinsed and drained
grated rind and juice of 1 lemon
30ml/2 tbsp olive oil
1 garlic clove, finely chopped
30ml/2 tbsp chopped fresh parsley
Tabasco sauce, to taste
cayenne pepper
salt and ground black pepper
chopped fresh parsley, to garnish

1 Put the beans in a shallow bowl and break them up coarsely with a potato masher.

2 Stir in the lemon rind and juice and olive oil, then the chopped garlic and parsley. Add Tabasco sauce, salt and black pepper to taste.

3 Spoon the mixture into a small bowl, dust lightly with cayenne and sprinkle with parsley. Chill until ready to serve.

Vegetarian Tapenade

This famous black olive paste usually contains anchovies, but the vegetarian version is just as delicious.

Serves 4
350g/12oz/3 cups pitted black olives
5 pieces of sun-dried tomatoes in oil, drained
30ml/2 tbsp drained capers
1–2 garlic cloves, coarsely chopped
5ml/1 tsp chopped fresh thyme
15ml/1 tbsp Dijon mustard
juice of 1/2 lemon
45ml/3 tbsp olive oil

1 Place all the ingredients in a food processor. Process to a smooth purée, then scrape into a serving dish. Cover and chill slightly before serving.

Chilli Bean Dip

This creamy bean dip is best served warm with grilled pitta bread.

Serves 4
30ml/2 tbsp vegetable oil
2 garlic cloves, crushed
1 onion, finely chopped
2 fresh green chillies, seeded and finely chopped
5–10ml/1–2 tsp hot chilli powder
400g/14oz can kidney beans
75g/3oz/ 3/4 cup grated mature (sharp) Cheddar cheese, plus extra to garnish
1 fresh red chilli, seeded
salt and ground black pepper
fresh green chillies, to garnish
triangles of grilled (broiled) pitta bread, to serve

1 Heat the oil in a deep, heavy frying pan. Add the garlic, onion, green chillies and chilli powder and cook over a low heat, stirring frequently, for about 5 minutes, until the onions are softened and transparent, but not browned.

2 Drain the kidney beans, reserving the can juices. Set aside 30ml/2 tbsp of the beans and put the remainder in a food processor. Process to a purée.

3 Add the puréed beans to the onion mixture and moisten with 30–45ml/2–3 tbsp of the reserved can juices. Heat gently, stirring to mix well.

4 Stir in the reserved whole kidney beans and the grated Cheddar. Cook over a low heat, stirring constantly, for 2–3 minutes, until the cheese has melted. Season to taste.

5 Cut the red chilli into thin strips. Spoon the dip into four individual serving bowls and sprinkle the chilli strips and extra cheese over the top. Serve warm, with the pitta triangles, garnished with green chillies.

Cook's Tip
For a dip with a coarser texture, do not purée the beans; instead, mash them with a potato masher.

Baba Ganoush with Lebanese Flatbread

Baba Ganoush is a delectable aubergine dip from the Middle East.

Serves 6
2 small aubergines
   (eggplant), halved
1 garlic clove, crushed
60ml/4 tbsp tahini
25g/1oz/ ¼ cup ground almonds
juice of ½ lemon
2.5ml/ ½ tsp ground cumin
30ml/2 tbsp fresh mint leaves
olive oil, for drizzling
salt and ground black pepper

For the Lebanese flatbread
4 pitta breads
45ml/3 tbsp toasted
   sesame seeds
45ml/3 tbsp chopped fresh
   thyme leaves
45ml/3 tbsp poppy seeds
150ml/ ¼ pint/ ⅔ cup olive oil

1 Make the flatbread. Split the pitta breads through the middle and carefully open them out. Mix the sesame seeds, thyme and poppy seeds in a mortar and crush them lightly with a pestle.

2 Stir in the olive oil. Spread the mixture lightly over the cut sides of the pitta bread. Grill (broil) until golden brown and crisp. When cool, break into coarse pieces and set aside.

3 Place the aubergines, skin side up, on a grill (broiler) rack and grill (broil) until the skins have blistered and charred. Transfer to a bowl, cover with crumpled kitchen paper and leave to cool for 10 minutes. Peel the aubergines, chop the flesh coarsely and leave it to drain in a colander.

4 Squeeze out as much liquid from the aubergines as possible. Place the flesh in a blender or food processor. Add the garlic, tahini, ground almonds, lemon juice and cumin and process to a smooth paste. Coarsely chop half the mint and stir it into the dip. Season to taste with salt and pepper.

5 Spoon the dip into a serving bowl, sprinkle the remaining mint on top and drizzle lightly with olive oil. Serve the dip with the Lebanese flatbread.

Lemon & Coconut Dhal

A warm spicy dish, this is perfect with poppadums or can be served as a main-meal accompaniment.

Serves 8
30ml/2 tbsp sunflower oil
5cm/2in piece of fresh root
   ginger, chopped
1 onion, chopped
2 garlic cloves, crushed
2 small fresh red chillies, seeded
   and chopped
5ml/1 tsp cumin seeds
150g/5oz/ ⅔ cup red lentils
250ml/8fl oz/1 cup water
15ml/1 tbsp hot curry paste
200ml/7fl oz/scant 1 cup
   coconut cream
juice of 1 lemon
handful of fresh coriander
   (cilantro) leaves
25g/1oz/ ¼ cup flaked
   (sliced) almonds
salt and ground black pepper
a few thin slices of red chilli,
   to garnish
poppadums, to serve

1 Heat the sunflower oil in a large, shallow pan. Add the ginger, onion, garlic, red chillies and cumin seeds. Cook over a medium heat, stirring occasionally, for about 5 minutes, until the onion is softened but not coloured.

2 Stir the lentils, water and curry paste into the pan and bring to the boil. Lower the heat, cover and cook for 15–20 minutes, stirring occasionally, until the lentils are just tender.

3 Stir in all but 30ml/2 tbsp of the coconut cream. Bring to the boil and cook, uncovered, for a further 15–20 minutes, until the mixture is thick and pulpy. Remove the pan from the heat, then stir in the lemon juice and the whole coriander leaves. Season with salt and pepper to taste.

4 Heat a large, heavy frying pan. Add the flaked almonds and dry-fry briefly over a medium heat, stirring frequently, until golden brown. Stir about three-quarters of the toasted almonds into the dhal.

5 Transfer the dhal to a serving bowl and swirl in the remaining coconut cream. Sprinkle the remaining toasted almonds and chilli slices on top. Serve warm, with poppadums.

Chilled Stuffed Courgettes

Full of flavour but low in calories and fat, this makes a superb summer appetizer.

Serves 6

6 courgettes (zucchini), trimmed
1 Spanish (Bermuda) onion, very finely chopped
1 garlic clove, crushed
60–90ml/4–6 tbsp well-flavoured French dressing
1 green (bell) pepper, seeded and diced
3 tomatoes, peeled, seeded and diced
15ml/1 tbsp drained and chopped rinsed capers
5ml/1 tsp chopped fresh parsley
5ml/1 tsp chopped fresh basil
sea salt and ground black pepper
fresh parsley sprigs, to garnish

1 Bring a large, shallow pan of lightly salted water to the boil. Add the courgettes and simmer for 2–3 minutes, until they are lightly cooked. Drain well.

2 Cut the courgettes in half lengthways. Carefully scoop out the flesh, leaving the courgette shells intact. Chop the flesh into small cubes. Place in a bowl and cover with half the chopped onion. Dot with the crushed garlic.

3 Drizzle 30ml/2 tbsp of the dressing over, cover and marinate for 2–3 hours. Wrap the courgette shells tightly in clear film (plastic wrap) and chill them until they are required.

4 Stir the pepper, tomatoes and capers into the courgette mixture, with the remaining onion and the herbs. Season to taste with sea salt and pepper. Pour over enough of the remaining dressing to moisten the mixture, toss well and chill.

5 Spoon the filling into the courgette shells, arrange on a platter and serve garnished with parsley.

Cook's Tip
To make French dressing, whisk together 15ml/1 tbsp wine vinegar, 5ml/1 tsp Dijon mustard and 75ml/5 tbsp olive oil.

Stuffed Mushrooms

This is a classic mushroom dish, strongly flavoured with garlic. Use flat or field (portabello) mushrooms.

Serves 6
12 large or 18 medium flat mushrooms
butter, for greasing
45ml/3 tbsp olive oil
2 garlic cloves, very finely chopped
45ml/3 tbsp finely chopped fresh parsley
40–50g/1½–2oz/¾–1 cup fresh white breadcrumbs
salt and ground black pepper
fresh flat leaf parsley sprig, to garnish

1 Preheat the oven to 180°C/350°F/Gas 4. Cut off the mushroom stalks and set them aside. Grease a shallow ovenproof dish with butter. Arrange the mushroom caps, gill side upwards, in the dish.

2 Heat 15ml/1 tbsp of the olive oil in a frying pan and cook the garlic briefly. Chop the mushroom stalks finely and mix them with the parsley and breadcrumbs. Add the garlic and 15ml/1 tbsp of the remaining oil and season with salt and pepper to taste. Mix thoroughly, then pile a little of the mixture on each mushroom cap.

3 Drizzle the remaining oil over the mushrooms, then cover them with buttered greaseproof (waxed) paper. Bake them for 15–20 minutes, removing the paper for the last 5 minutes.

4 Serve two or three mushrooms per portion, garnishing with flat leaf parsley.

Cook's Tips
• The cooking time for the mushroom caps depends on their size and thickness. If they are fairly thin, cook for slightly less time. They should be tender, but not too soft when cooked. Test them with the point of a sharp knife.
• If you like a stronger garlic flavour, do not cook the garlic before adding it to the breadcrumb mixture.

Pear & Parmesan Salad with Poppy Seed Dressing

This is a good appetizer when pears are at their seasonal best. Drizzle them with a poppy-seed dressing and top them with shavings of Parmesan cheese.

Serves 4

4 just-ripe pears
50g/2oz piece of
    Parmesan cheese
watercress, to garnish
water biscuits (crackers) or rye
    bread, to serve (optional)

For the dressing

30ml/2 tbsp cider vinegar
2.5ml/ 1/2 tsp soft light
    brown sugar
good pinch of dried thyme
30ml/2 tbsp extra virgin olive oil
15ml/1 tbsp sunflower oil
15ml/1 tbsp poppy seeds
salt and ground black pepper

1 Peel the pears if you like, although they look more attractive with the skin on. Cut them in quarters and remove the cores.

2 Cut each pear quarter in half lengthways and arrange them on four small serving plates.

3 Make the dressing. Mix the vinegar, sugar and thyme in a jug (pitcher). Gradually whisk in the olive oil, then the sunflower oil. Season with salt and pepper, then tip in the poppy seeds.

4 Trickle the dressing over the pears. Shave Parmesan over the top and garnish with watercress. Serve with water biscuits or thinly sliced rye bread, if you like.

> **Variation**
> Blue cheeses and pears also have a natural affinity. Stilton, dolcelatte, Gorgonzola or Danish blue can be used instead of the shavings of Parmesan. Allow about 200g/7oz and cut into wedges or cubes.

Dressed Salad of Fresh Ceps

Mushrooms make a marvellous salad, especially if you are able to obtain fresh ceps or bay boletus. Any wild or cultivated mushrooms can be used; remove the stems from shiitake mushrooms.

Serves 4

350g/12oz/4 cups fresh ceps or
    bay boletus, thinly sliced
175g/6oz ready-to-serve mixed
    salad leaves
50g/2oz/ 1/2 cup broken walnut
    pieces, toasted

50g/2oz piece of
    Parmesan cheese
salt and ground black pepper

For the dressing

2 egg yolks
2.5ml/ 1/2 tsp French mustard
75ml/5 tbsp groundnut
    (peanut) oil
45ml/3 tbsp walnut oil
30ml/2 tbsp lemon juice
30ml/2 tbsp chopped
    fresh parsley
pinch of caster (superfine) sugar

1 Make the dressing. Place the egg yolks in a screw-top jar with the mustard, groundnut oil, walnut oil, lemon juice, parsley and sugar. Close the jar tightly and shake well.

2 Place the mushrooms in a large salad bowl and pour over the dressing. Toss to coat, then set aside for 10–15 minutes.

3 Add the salad leaves to the mushrooms and toss lightly. Season with plenty of salt and pepper.

4 Divide the salad among four large plates. Sprinkle each portion with toasted walnuts and shavings of Parmesan cheese.

> **Cook's Tip**
> The dressing for this salad uses raw egg yolks. Be sure to use only the freshest eggs from a reputable supplier. Expectant mothers, young children and the elderly are advised to avoid raw egg yolks. If this presents a problem, the dressing can be made without the egg yolks.

Split Tin Loaf

As its name suggests, this basic loaf is so called because of the centre split. Some bakers mould the dough in two loaves which join together when the dough is set aside to rise, but retain the characteristic crack after baking.

Makes 1 loaf
500g/1¼lb/5 cups unbleached
    strong white bread flour, plus
    extra for dusting
10ml/2 tsp salt
15g/½oz fresh yeast
300ml/½ pint/1¼ cups
    lukewarm water
60ml/4 tbsp lukewarm milk

1 Lightly grease a 900g/2lb loaf tin (pan). Sift the flour and salt into a bowl and make a well in the centre. Mix the yeast with half the water in a jug (pitcher), then stir in the remaining water.

2 Pour the yeast mixture into the centre of the flour. Gradually mix in enough of the surrounding flour to make a thick, smooth batter. Sprinkle a little more flour over the batter and leave in a warm place for about 20 minutes, until bubbles appear in the batter. Add the milk and remaining flour. Mix to a firm dough.

3 Knead on a lightly floured surface for 10 minutes, until smooth and elastic. Place in a lightly oiled bowl, cover with lightly oiled clear film (plastic wrap) and set aside in a warm place for 1–1¼ hours, or until nearly doubled in bulk.

4 Knock back (punch down) the dough, then shape it into a rectangle the length of the tin. Roll up lengthways, tuck the ends under and place, seam side down, in the tin. Cover and leave in a warm place for 20–30 minutes, or until nearly doubled in size.

5 Using a sharp knife, make one deep central slash the length of the bread, then dust with flour. Leave for 10–15 minutes. Preheat the oven to 230°C/450°F/Gas 8.

6 Bake for 15 minutes, then reduce the oven temperature to 200°C/400°F/Gas 6. Bake for 20–25 minutes more, or until the bread is golden and sounds hollow when tapped on the base. Turn out on to a wire rack to cool.

Grant Loaves

The dough for these quick and easy loaves requires no kneading and takes only a minute to mix.

Makes 3 loaves
oil, for greasing
1.3kg/3lb/12 cups strong
    wholemeal (whole-wheat)
    bread flour

15ml/1 tbsp salt
15ml/1 tbsp easy-blend (rapid-
    rise) dried yeast
15ml/1 tbsp muscovado
    (molasses) sugar
1.2 litres/2 pints/5 cups
    lukewarm water

1 Thoroughly grease three loaf tins (pans), each measuring about 21 x 12 x 6cm/8½ x 4½ x 2½in and set aside in a warm place. Sift the flour and salt into a large bowl and warm slightly. Stir in the yeast and sugar. Make a well in the centre and pour in the water. Mix for about 1 minute, working the sides into the middle. The dough should be slippery.

2 Divide among the prepared tins, cover with oiled clear film (plastic wrap) and leave in a warm place, for 30 minutes, or until the dough has risen to within about 1cm/½in of the top of the tins.

3 Meanwhile, preheat the oven to 200°C/400°F/Gas 6. Bake for 40 minutes, or until the loaves are crisp and sound hollow when tapped on the base. Cool on a wire rack.

Cook's Tips
• *Most breads require a raising or leavening agent, and yeast is the commonest, although there are a number of others.*
• *Easy-blend (rapid-rise) dried yeast is widely available. There is no need to mix it with liquid before adding it to the flour and other dry ingredients. Lukewarm liquid is then added.*
• *Ordinary dried yeast must be mixed with a little warm liquid, and sometimes with sugar as well. When it has dissolved and the mixture is frothy, it can be added to the dried ingredients.*

Sour Rye Bread

You need to plan ahead to make this loaf, as the starter takes a day or two.

Makes 2 loaves
450g/1lb/4 cups rye flour
450g/1lb/4 cups strong white
  bread flour, plus extra
  for dusting
15ml/1 tbsp salt
7g/ 1/4oz sachet easy-blend
  (rapid-rise) dried yeast

25g/1oz/2 tbsp butter, softened
600ml/1 pint/2 1/2 cups
  lukewarm water
vegetable oil, for greasing
15ml/1 tbsp caraway seeds,
  for sprinkling

For the sourdough starter
60ml/4 tbsp rye flour
45ml/3 tbsp warm milk

1 For the sourdough starter, mix the rye flour and milk in a small bowl. Cover with clear film (plastic wrap) and leave in a warm place for 1–2 days, or until it smells pleasantly sour.

2 Sift both types of flour and the salt into a large bowl and stir in the yeast. Make a well in the centre and add the butter, water and sourdough starter. Mix to a soft dough.

3 Knead the dough on a floured surface for 10 minutes. Put it in a clean bowl, cover with lightly oiled clear film and leave in a warm place to rise for 1 hour, or until doubled in bulk.

4 Knead for 1 minute. Divide the dough in half. Shape each piece into a 15cm/6in round. Place on greased baking sheets. Cover with oiled clear film and leave to rise for 30 minutes.

5 Preheat the oven to 200°C/400°F/Gas 6. Brush the loaves with water, sprinkle with caraway seeds and bake them for 35–40 minutes, until browned. Cool on a wire rack.

> **Cook's Tip**
> *Sour rye bread keeps fresh for up to a week. This recipe can also be made without yeast, but it will be much denser.*

Pan de Cebada

This Spanish bread is perfect for serving with chilled soup or a healthy dip.

Makes 1 large loaf
For the sourdough starter
175g/6oz/1 1/2 cups maize
  meal (cornmeal)
560ml/scant 1 pint/scant
  2 1/2 cups water
225g/8oz/2 cups strong
  wholemeal (whole-wheat) bread
  flour, plus extra

75g/3oz/ 3/4 cup barley flour
vegetable oil, for greasing

For the dough
maize meal (cornmeal),
  for dusting
20g/ 3/4oz fresh yeast
45ml/3 tbsp lukewarm water
225g/8oz/2 cups strong
  wholemeal (whole-wheat)
  bread flour
15ml/1 tbsp salt

1 In a pan, mix the maize meal for the sourdough starter with half the water, then stir in the remainder. Stir over a low heat until thickened. Transfer to a bowl and set aside to cool. Mix in the wholemeal and barley flours. Knead on a lightly floured surface for 5 minutes, then return to the bowl, cover with oiled clear film (plastic wrap) and leave in a warm place for 36 hours.

2 Make the dough. Dust a baking sheet with maize meal. In a small bowl, cream the yeast with the water, then add to the starter with the wholemeal flour and salt and work to a dough. Knead on a lightly floured surface for 4–5 minutes. Put the dough in a lightly oiled bowl, cover with oiled clear film and leave in a warm place to rise for 1 1/2–2 hours.

3 Knock back (punch down) the dough, shape it into a plump round and sprinkle with a little maize meal. Place on the baking sheet and cover with a large upturned bowl. Leave in a warm place to rise for about 1 hour, or until nearly doubled in bulk.

4 Place a roasting pan in the oven and preheat to 220°C/425°F/Gas 7. Pour 300ml/ 1/2 pint/1 1/4 cups water into the pan. Lift the bowl off the loaf and bake the loaf for 10 minutes. Remove the pan of water, lower the temperature to 190°C/375°F/Gas 5 and bake for 20 minutes more. Cool on a rack.

Spiral Herb Bread

When cut, this loaf looks very pretty with its swirls of garlic and herbs.

Makes 2 loaves
350g/12oz/3 cups strong white bread flour, plus extra for dusting
350g/12oz/3 cups strong wholemeal (whole-wheat) bread flour
2 x 7g/¼oz sachets easy-blend (rapid-rise) dried yeast
600ml/1 pint/2½ cups lukewarm water
vegetable oil, for greasing
25g/1oz/2 tbsp butter
1 bunch of spring onions (scallions), finely chopped
1 garlic clove, finely chopped
1 large bunch of fresh parsley, finely chopped
1 egg, lightly beaten
salt and ground black pepper
milk, for glazing

1 Mix the flours in a large bowl. Stir in 15ml/1 tbsp salt and the yeast. Make a well in the centre and pour in the water. Beat, gradually incorporating the flour to make a coarse dough. Knead the dough on a floured surface for 8–10 minutes. Return it to the bowl, cover with lightly oiled clear film (plastic wrap) and leave in a warm place for 2 hours, until doubled in bulk.

2 Meanwhile, melt the butter in a pan and cook the spring onions and garlic over a low heat, until softened. Season with salt and pepper, stir in the parsley and set aside.

3 Grease two 23 x 13cm/9 x 5in loaf tins (pans). When the dough has risen, cut it in half, then roll each half to a 35 x 23cm/14 x 9in rectangle. Brush with the beaten egg and divide the herb mixture between them, spreading it just to the edges. Roll up each dough rectangle from a long side and pinch the short ends together to seal. Place in the tins, seam side down. Cover and leave in a warm place until the dough has risen above the rims of the tins.

4 Preheat the oven to 190°C/375°F/Gas 5. Brush the loaves with milk and bake for 55 minutes, until they are golden and sound hollow when tapped on the base. Cool on a wire rack.

Three-grain Twist

A mixture of grains gives this close-textured bread a delightful nutty flavour.

Makes 1 loaf
30ml/2 tbsp malt extract
475ml/16fl oz/2 cups boiling water
225g/8oz/2 cups strong white bread flour, plus extra for dusting
7.5ml/1½ tsp salt
225g/8oz/2 cups malted brown flour
225g/8oz/2 cups rye flour
15ml/1 tbsp easy-blend (rapid rise) dried yeast
pinch of granulated sugar
30ml/2 tbsp linseed
75g/3oz/scant 1 cup medium oatmeal
45ml/3 tbsp sunflower seeds
vegetable oil, for greasing

1 Stir the malt extract into the boiling water. Let the mixture cool until it is lukewarm.

2 Sift the white flour and salt into a mixing bowl and add the other flours. Stir in the yeast and sugar. Set aside 5ml/1 tsp of the linseed and add the rest to the flour mixture with the oatmeal and sunflower seeds. Make a well in the centre.

3 Pour the malted water into the well and gradually mix in the flour to make a soft dough, adding extra water if necessary. Knead on a floured surface for about 5 minutes, then return to the clean bowl, cover with lightly oiled clear film (plastic wrap) and leave in a warm place for 2 hours until doubled in bulk.

4 Flour a baking sheet. Knead the dough again and divide it in half. Roll each half to a 30cm/12in long sausage. Twist them together, dampen the ends and press to seal. Lift the twist on to the baking sheet. Brush it with water, sprinkle with the remaining linseed and cover loosely with a large plastic bag. Leave in a warm place until well risen. Preheat the oven to 220°C/425°F/Gas 7.

5 Bake the loaf for 10 minutes, then reduce the temperature to 200°C/400°F/Gas 6 and cook for 20 minutes more, or until the loaf sounds hollow when it is tapped. Cool on a wire rack.

Tomato Breadsticks

Fresh, healthy and low in fat, these are delectable with dips. Make plenty, as they are very moreish.

Makes 16
225g/8oz/2 cups plain (all-purpose) flour, plus extra for dusting
2.5ml/ ½ tsp salt
7.5ml/1½ tsp easy-blend (rapid-rise) dried yeast
5ml/1 tsp clear honey
10ml/2 tsp olive oil, plus extra about 150ml/ ¼ pint/ ⅔ cup lukewarm water
6 pieces of sun-dried tomatoes in olive oil, drained and chopped
15ml/1 tbsp skimmed milk
10ml/2 tsp poppy seeds

1 Place the flour, salt and yeast in a food processor. Add the honey and 5ml/1 tsp of the olive oil and, with the machine running, gradually pour in enough lukewarm water to make a dough. Process for 1 minute more.

2 Knead the dough on a lightly floured surface for 3–4 minutes. Knead in the chopped sun-dried tomatoes. Form the dough into a ball and place in a lightly oiled bowl. Set aside to rise for 5 minutes.

3 Preheat the oven to 150°C/300°F/Gas 2. Lightly brush a baking sheet with oil.

4 Divide the dough into 16 pieces and roll each piece into a stick about 28 × 1cm/11 × ½in. Place the breadsticks on the prepared baking sheet and set aside in a warm place to rise for 15 minutes.

5 Brush the sticks with milk and sprinkle with poppy seeds. Bake for 30 minutes. Cool on a wire rack.

Cook's Tip
Flours vary in their absorbency, so you may not require all the water. Stop adding it as soon as soon as the dough starts to cling together.

Wholemeal Herb Triangles

Stuffed with salad and cheese, these make a good lunchtime snack.

Makes 8
225g/8oz/2 cups wholemeal (whole-wheat) flour, plus extra for dusting
115g/4oz/1 cup strong white bread flour
5ml/1 tsp salt
2.5ml/ ½ tsp bicarbonate of soda (baking soda)
5ml/1 tsp cream of tartar
2.5ml/ ½ tsp chilli powder
50g/2oz/ ¼ cup soft margarine
60ml/4 tbsp chopped mixed fresh herbs
250ml/8fl oz/1 cup skimmed milk
15ml/1 tbsp sesame seeds

1 Preheat the oven to 220°C/425°F/Gas 7. Lightly flour a baking sheet. Put the wholemeal flour in a mixing bowl. Sift in the white flour, salt, soda, cream of tartar and chilli powder, then rub in the soft margarine.

2 Add the herbs and milk and mix quickly to a soft dough. Turn on to a lightly floured surface. Knead only very briefly.

3 Roll out to a 23cm/9in round and place on the prepared baking sheet. Brush lightly with water and sprinkle evenly with the sesame seeds.

4 Carefully cut the dough round into 8 wedges, separate them slightly and bake for 15–20 minutes. Cool briefly on a wire rack and serve warm.

Variations
• *For cheese and herb triangles, add 50–115g/2–4oz/½–1 cup grated Gruyère or Emmenthal cheese after rubbing in the margarine in step 1.*
• *To make sun-dried tomato triangles, omit the fresh mixed herbs and replace them with 30ml/2 tbsp drained chopped sun-dried tomatoes in oil. Add 15ml/1 tbsp each mild paprika, chopped fresh parsley and chopped fresh marjoram with the milk in step 2.*

Cheese & Mustard Scones

Depending on their size, these cheese scones can be served as little canapé bases, after-school treats or even as a quick pie topping.

Makes 12
250g/9oz/2¼ cups self-raising (self-rising) flour, plus extra for dusting
5ml/1 tsp baking powder
2.5ml/½ tsp salt
40g/1½oz/3 tbsp butter
175g/6oz/1½ cups grated mature (sharp) Cheddar cheese, plus extra for sprinkling
10ml/2 tsp wholegrain mustard
about 150ml/¼ pint/⅔ cup milk
ground black pepper

To serve (optional)
garlic-flavoured cream cheese
chopped fresh chives
sliced radishes

1 Preheat the oven to 220°C/425°F/Gas 7. Sift the flour, baking powder and salt into a large bowl, then rub in the butter with your fingertips. Season to taste with pepper and stir in the grated cheese.

2 Mix the mustard with the milk until thoroughly combined. Add the mixture to the dry ingredients and mix quickly until the mixture just comes together.

3 Knead the dough lightly on a lightly floured surface, then pat it out to a depth of 2cm/¾in. Use a 5cm/2in cutter to stamp out rounds. Place on a non-stick baking sheet and sprinkle with extra grated cheese.

4 Bake for 10 minutes, until risen and golden. You can test scones by pressing the sides, which should spring back. Cool on a wire rack. Serve spread with garlic-flavoured cream cheese, topped with chopped chives and sliced radishes, if you like.

> **Cook's Tip**
> *Do not over-mix the dough, or the scones will be heavy, tough and chewy.*

Sunflower & Almond Sesame Crackers

Full of flavour, these slim savoury crackers taste great with cheese and celery, or could be served with hummus or a similar dip.

Makes about 24
130g/4½oz/1 cup ground sunflower seeds
90g/3½oz/scant 1 cup ground almonds
5ml/1 tsp baking powder
30ml/2 tbsp milk
1 egg yolk
25g/1oz/2 tbsp butter, melted
25g/1oz/¼ cup sesame seeds

1 Preheat the oven to 190°C/375°F/Gas 5. Reserve 25g/1oz/¼ cup of the ground sunflower seeds for rolling out and mix the remaining ground seeds with the ground almonds and baking powder in a bowl.

2 Mix the milk and egg yolk in a cup, then stir the mixture into the dry ingredients, with the melted butter, mixing well. Gently work the mixture with your hands to form a moist dough.

3 On a cool surface that has been lightly dusted with some of the reserved ground sunflower seeds, roll out the dough to a thickness of about 5mm/¼in, sprinkling more ground seeds on top to prevent sticking.

4 Sprinkle the dough with sesame seeds and cut into rounds, with a 5cm/2in pastry cutter. Lift on to a non-stick baking sheet.

5 Bake the crackers for about 10 minutes, until lightly browned. Cool on a wire rack.

> **Variation**
> *Sprinkle some poppy seeds on top of a few of the crackers before baking.*

Oatcakes

Old-fashioned they may be, but oatcakes are delicious, especially with cheese.

Makes 8
175g/6oz/1 1/2 cups medium
  oatmeal, plus extra
  for sprinkling
2.5ml/1/2 tsp salt
pinch of bicarbonate of soda
  (baking soda)
15g/ 1/2oz/1 tbsp butter, plus
  extra for greasing
75ml/5 tbsp water

1 Preheat the oven to 150°C/300°F/Gas 2. Mix the oatmeal with the salt and bicarbonate of soda in a mixing bowl.

2 Melt the butter with the water in a small pan. Bring to the boil, then add to the oatmeal mixture and mix thoroughly to form a moist dough.

3 Turn the dough on to a surface sprinkled with oatmeal and knead to a smooth ball. Turn a large baking sheet upside down, grease it, sprinkle it lightly with oatmeal and place the ball of dough on top. Sprinkle the dough with oatmeal, then roll out to a 25cm/10in round.

4 Cut the round into eight sections, ease them apart slightly and bake for 50–60 minutes, until crisp. Leave to cool on the baking sheet, then remove the oatcakes with a spatula.

Cook's Tips
• To achieve a neat round, place a 25cm/10in cake board or plate on top of the oatcake. Cut away any excess dough with a palette knife or metal spatula, then lift off the board or plate.
• Oatmeal is ground from the whole kernel of the cereal and is graded according to how finely it is ground. The largest and coarsest type is pinhead, then, in descending order of size, rough, medium, fine and superfine. Medium oatmeal is widely available, but fine is also suitable for oatcakes. Oat flakes, made from steamed rolled oats, are not suitable.

Rosemary Crackers

Rosemary is said to grow best for a strong-willed woman. If you have some in your garden, make these excellent crackers and top them with cream cheese and rosemary flowers.

Makes about 25
225g/8oz/2 cups plain (all-
  purpose) flour
2.5ml/ 1/2 tsp baking powder
a good pinch of salt
2.5ml/ 1/2 tsp curry powder
75g/3oz/6 tbsp butter, diced
30ml/2 tbsp finely chopped young
  rosemary leaves
1 egg yolk
30–45ml/2–3 tbsp water
milk, to glaze

To decorate
30ml/2 tbsp cream cheese
rosemary flowers

1 Put the flour, baking powder, salt and curry powder in a food processor. Add the butter and process until the mixture resembles fine breadcrumbs. Add the rosemary, egg yolk and 30ml/2 tbsp of the water. Process again, adding the remaining water, if needed, to make a firm dough. Wrap in clear film (plastic wrap) and chill in the refrigerator for 30 minutes.

2 Preheat the oven to 180°C/350°F/Gas 4. Roll out the dough thinly on a lightly floured surface and cut out the crackers using a 5cm/2in fluted cutter.

3 Transfer them to a large baking sheet and prick with a fork. Brush with milk to glaze and bake for about 10 minutes, until pale golden. Cool on a wire rack.

4 Spread a little cream cheese on to each cracker and secure a few rosemary flowers on top, using tweezers to position the flowers, if this makes it easier.

Cook's Tip
If you do not have a food processor, simply rub the butter into the flour mixture in a bowl, then add the remaining ingredients and combine.

MEALS IN MINUTES

The demands on our time these days seem to be ever increasing and, happily, this chapter is packed with a wealth of irresistible nutritious dishes that can be prepared and cooked in next to no time. Whether you need a family supper or a quick meal for just one or two people, you are sure to find a speedy dish to please.

As the Chinese virtually invented fast food, it is hardly surprising that this chapter features a mouthwatering collection of stir-fries. The variety is immense, from Spring Vegetable Stir-fry to Stir-fried Chickpeas. As if all this is not enough, stir-fries also have the additional advantage of being one-pot dishes, so you won't have to spend very much time clearing up afterwards.

The Indian sub-continent has also inspired a number of the recipes. A large percentage of the Indian population is vegetarian so, over the years, generations of Indian cooks have achieved the perfect balance of spices and herbs to complement vegetables and pulses. Not all of the dishes are searingly hot, so you will find something to suit all tastes, from the delicately aromatic Vegetable Kashmiri to the rather more fiery Aloo Saag.

Most Western cuisines also include their own fast-food specialities. Pasta is always a favourite with young and old alike and it is particularly good when partnered with vegetables or mushrooms, for example, Mushroom Bolognese. Eggs are probably the ultimate convenience food for quick cooking. Boiled or scrambled in minutes, they provide an almost instant snack when you are feeling peckish. However, hardly any more effort or time is required to make something a little more special. Soufflé Omelette with Mushrooms is the versatile solution to the common problem of family members who want or need to eat at different times.

Spring Vegetable Stir-fry

A dazzling and colourful medley of fresh and sweet young vegetables.

Serves 4
15ml/1 tbsp groundnut (peanut) oil
1 garlic clove, sliced
2.5cm/1in piece of fresh root ginger, finely chopped
115g/4oz baby carrots
115g/4oz small patty pan squash
115g/4oz baby corn cobs
115g/4oz green beans, trimmed
115g/4oz sugar snap peas, trimmed
115g/4oz young asparagus, cut into 7.5cm/3in pieces
8 spring onions (scallions), trimmed and cut into 5cm/2in pieces
115g/4oz cherry tomatoes

For the dressing
juice of 2 limes
15ml/1 tbsp clear honey
15ml/1 tbsp soy sauce
5ml/1 tsp sesame oil

1 Heat the groundnut oil in a wok and stir-fry the garlic and ginger over a high heat for 30 seconds.

2 Reduce the heat to medium and add the baby carrots, patty pan squash, corn cobs and green beans and stir-fry for 3–4 minutes more.

3 Add the sugar snap peas, asparagus, spring onions and cherry tomatoes. Toss over the heat for a further 1–2 minutes.

4 Mix the dressing ingredients in a jug (pitcher) and pour them over the vegetables. Stir well, cover and cook for 2–3 minutes more, until the vegetables are crisp-tender. Serve immediately.

> **Variation**
> *You can use any seasonal vegetables, provided they are tender enough to cook quickly. Cauliflower or broccoli florets, (bell) pepper strips, mangetouts (snow peas) and sliced courgettes (zucchini) would all be suitable. Make sure they are cut into similar size pieces so that they cook simultaneously. Add thinly sliced red onion and celery when frying the garlic, if you like.*

Lentil Stir-fry

Mushrooms, artichokes, sugar snap peas and lentils make a satisfying stir-fry for a speedy supper.

Serves 2–3
115g/4oz sugar snap peas
25g/1oz/2 tbsp butter
1 small onion, chopped
115g/4oz/1½ cups cup or brown cap (cremini) mushrooms, sliced
400g/14oz can artichoke hearts, drained and halved
400g/14oz can cooked green lentils, drained
60ml/4 tbsp single (light) cream
25g/1oz/¼ cup flaked (sliced) almonds, toasted
salt and ground black pepper
French bread, to serve

1 Bring a pan of lightly salted water to the boil and cook the sugar snap peas for 4 minutes, or until just tender. Drain, refresh under cold running water, then drain again. Pat them dry with kitchen paper and set them aside.

2 Melt the butter in a large, heavy frying pan. Add the chopped onion and cook over a medium heat, stirring occasionally for 2–3 minutes, until beginning to soften.

3 Stir in the sliced mushrooms, then cook, stirring occasionally, for 2–3 minutes, until just tender. Add the artichoke hearts, sugar snap peas and lentils to the pan. Stir-fry over a medium heat for 2 minutes.

4 Stir in the cream and almonds and cook for 1 minute. Season to taste. Serve immediately, with chunks of French bread.

> **Cook's Tip**
> *Canned lentils are convenient, but it doesn't take long to cook dried lentils. Unlike most pulses, they don't need soaking. To add flavour, simmer them in vegetable stock or water to which you have added a little yeast extract. Do not add salt, as this tends to make the lentils tough. They will take 20–30 minutes, depending on type and the degree of freshness.*

Balti Stir-fried Vegetables with Cashews

This versatile stir-fry recipe will accommodate most other combinations of vegetables – you do not have to use the selection suggested here.

Serves 4

2 carrots
1 red (bell) pepper, seeded
1 green (bell) pepper, seeded
2 courgettes (zucchini)
115g/4oz green beans, halved
1 bunch spring onions (scallions)
15ml/1 tbsp virgin olive oil
4–6 curry leaves
2.5ml/ ½ tsp white cumin seeds
4 dried red chillies
10–12 cashew nuts
5ml/1 tsp salt
30ml/2 tbsp lemon juice
fresh mint leaves, to garnish

1 Prepare the vegetables: cut the carrots, peppers and courgettes into thin batons, halve the beans and chop the spring onions. Set aside.

2 Heat the oil in a wok and stir-fry the curry leaves, cumin seeds and dried chillies for 1 minute.

3 Add the vegetables and nuts and toss them over the heat for 3–4 minutes. Add the salt and lemon juice. Continue to stir and toss over the heat for 2 minutes more, or until the vegetables are crisp-tender.

4 Transfer to a warmed serving dish. Remove the dried chillies, if you like. Serve immediately, garnished with mint leaves.

Cook's Tips
• When making any of the stir-fries in this section, it is a good idea to use a non-stick wok to minimize the amount of oil needed. However, it cannot be heated to the same high temperature as a conventional wok.
• You can reduce the fat content still further by using a light oil cooking spray instead of the olive oil.

Carrot & Cauliflower Stir-fry

There's plenty of crunch in this tasty, quick-cooking supper dish, which is high in fibre, but very low in fat.

Serves 4

15ml/1 tbsp olive oil
1 bay leaf
2 cloves
1 small cinnamon stick
2 cardamom pods
3 black peppercorns
5ml/1 tsp salt
2 large carrots, cut into thin batons
1 small cauliflower, broken into florets
50g/2oz/ ½ cup frozen peas
10ml/2 tsp lemon juice
15ml/1 tbsp chopped fresh coriander (cilantro), plus extra leaves, to garnish

1 Heat the oil in a wok and add the bay leaf, cloves, cinnamon stick, cardamoms and peppercorns. Stir-fry over a medium heat for 30–35 seconds, then add the salt.

2 Add the carrot and cauliflower and stir-fry for 3–5 minutes. Add the peas, lemon juice and chopped coriander and cook for 2–3 minutes more. Serve, garnished with the coriander leaves.

Broccoli Stir-fry

Ginger and orange make this quick stir-fry deliciously tangy and flavoursome.

Serves 4

675g/1½lb broccoli, broken into florets
2 slices fresh root ginger
juice of 1 orange
10ml/2 tsp cornflour (cornstarch)
2.5ml/½ tsp sugar
60ml/4 tbsp water
15ml/1 tbsp olive oil
1 garlic clove, thinly sliced
thin strips of orange rind, soaked in cold water

1 Slice the broccoli stems and cut the ginger into thin batons. Mix the orange juice with the cornflour, sugar and water.
2 Heat the oil in a wok. Stir-fry the stems for 2 minutes. Add the ginger, garlic and florets and stir-fry for 3 minutes. Stir in the orange mixture until thickened. Toss in the rind and serve.

Mixed Vegetable Stir-fry

Serve this stir-fry with rice or noodles.

Serves 4

15ml/1 tbsp vegetable oil
5ml/1 tsp toasted sesame oil
1 garlic clove, chopped
2.5cm/1in piece of fresh root
   ginger, finely chopped
225g/8oz baby carrots

350g/12oz broccoli florets
175g/6oz asparagus tips
2 spring onions (scallions),
   cut diagonally
175g/6oz spring greens
   (collards), shredded
30ml/2 tbsp light soy sauce
15ml/1 tbsp apple juice
15ml/1 tbsp sesame
   seeds, toasted

1 Heat the oils in a wok and sauté the garlic over a low heat for 2 minutes. Raise the heat, add the ginger, carrots, broccoli and asparagus and stir-fry for 4 minutes. Add the spring onions and spring greens and stir-fry for 2 minutes.

2 Drizzle over the soy sauce and apple juice and toss for 1–2 minutes. Sprinkle the sesame seeds on top and serve.

Mixed Cabbage Stir-fry

Use three or four different types of cabbage, including pak choi.

Serves 4

15ml/1 tbsp vegetable oil
1 garlic clove, chopped
2.5cm/1in piece of fresh root
   ginger, finely chopped

450g/1lb mixed cabbage leaves,
   finely shredded
10ml/2 tsp light soy sauce
5ml/1 tsp clear honey
15ml/1 tbsp sesame
   seeds, toasted

1 Heat the oil in a wok and sauté the garlic over a low heat for 2 minutes. Raise the heat and add the ginger and shredded cabbage. Stir-fry for 4 minutes.
2 Drizzle over the soy sauce and honey and toss over the heat for 1–2 minutes. Sprinkle with the sesame seeds and serve.

Braised Aubergine & Courgettes

Fresh red chillies add a flicker of fire to a dish that is simple, spicy and quite sensational. If you don't like your food quite so hot, use mild chillies or even sweet red (bell) peppers.

Serves 4

1 aubergine (eggplant), about
   350g/12oz
2 small courgettes (zucchini)

15ml/1 tbsp vegetable oil
2 garlic cloves, finely chopped
2 fresh red chillies, seeded and
   finely chopped
1 small onion, diced
15ml/1 tbsp black bean sauce
15ml/1 tbsp dark soy sauce
45ml/3 tbsp water
salt

1 Trim the aubergine and slice it in half lengthways, then cut it across into 1cm/½in slices. Layer the slices in a colander, sprinkling each layer with salt. Leave the colander in the sink for about 20 minutes, so that the liquid that is drawn from the aubergine drains away.

2 Meanwhile, roll cut each courgette by slicing off one end diagonally, then rolling the courgette through 180° and taking off another diagonal slice to form a triangular wedge. Make more wedges of courgette in the same way.

3 Rinse the aubergine slices well under cold running water, drain and dry thoroughly on kitchen paper.

4 Heat the oil in a preheated wok. Add the finely chopped garlic, chopped chillies and diced onion and stir-fry over a medium heat for 2–3 minutes. Stir in the black bean sauce, coating the onions well.

5 Lower the heat and add the aubergine slices. Stir-fry for 2 minutes, sprinkling over a little water, if necessary, to prevent them from burning.

6 Stir in the courgettes, soy sauce and measured water. Cook, stirring occasionally, for 5 minutes. Serve hot.

Braised Tofu with Mushrooms

The mushrooms flavour the tofu to make this the perfect low-fat vegetarian main course.

Serves 4
350g/12oz firm tofu
2.5ml/ ½ tsp sesame oil
10ml/2 tsp light soy sauce
15ml/1 tbsp vegetable oil
2 garlic cloves, finely chopped
2.5ml/ ½ tsp grated fresh
 root ginger
115g/4oz/1½ cups shiitake
 mushrooms, stalks removed
175g/6oz/generous 2 cups
 oyster mushrooms
115g/4oz/1½ cups drained,
 canned straw mushrooms
115g/4oz/1½ cups button
 (white) mushrooms, cut in half
15ml/1 tbsp Chinese rice wine or
 medium-dry sherry
15ml/1 tbsp dark soy sauce
90ml/6 tbsp vegetable stock
5ml/1 tsp cornflour (cornstarch)
15ml/1 tbsp water
salt and ground white pepper
2 spring onions (scallions),
 shredded, to garnish

1 Put the tofu in a dish and sprinkle with the sesame oil, light soy sauce and a large pinch of pepper. Leave to marinate for 10 minutes, then drain and cut into 2.5 × 1cm/1 × ½in pieces, using a sharp knife.

2 Heat the vegetable oil in a wok. Add the garlic and ginger and stir-fry over a low heat for a few seconds. Raise the heat, add all the mushrooms and stir-fry for 2 minutes.

3 Stir in the Chinese rice wine or sherry, soy sauce and stock and season with salt and pepper to taste. Toss over the heat for about 4 minutes.

4 Mix the cornflour to a paste with the water. Stir the mixture into the wok and cook, stirring constantly, until thickened.

5 Carefully add the pieces of marinated tofu, toss gently to coat thoroughly and simmer for 2 minutes.

6 Transfer the stir-fry to a large, warmed serving dish and sprinkle the shredded spring onions over the top to garnish. Serve immediately.

Red-cooked Tofu with Chinese Mushrooms

Red-cooked is a term used for Chinese dishes cooked with dark soy sauce.

Serves 2–4
6 dried Chinese mushrooms
225g/8oz firm tofu
45ml/3 tbsp dark soy sauce
30ml/2 tbsp Chinese rice wine or
 medium-dry sherry
10ml/2 tsp soft dark brown sugar
1 garlic clove, crushed
15ml/1 tbsp grated fresh
 root ginger
2.5ml/ ½ tsp Chinese five-
 spice powder
pinch of ground roasted
 Sichuan peppercorns
5ml/1 tsp cornflour (cornstarch)
30ml/2 tbsp groundnut
 (peanut) oil
5–6 spring onions (scallions),
 sliced into short lengths
small fresh basil leaves, to garnish
cooked rice noodles, to serve

1 Soak the dried Chinese mushrooms in warm water for 20–30 minutes, until soft.

2 Meanwhile, cut the tofu into 2.5cm/1in cubes. Place in a shallow dish. Combine the soy sauce, rice wine or sherry, sugar, garlic, ginger, five-spice powder and Sichuan pepper. Pour this over the tofu, toss lightly and marinate for 10 minutes. Drain, reserve the marinade and stir in the cornflour.

3 Drain the mushrooms, reserving 90ml/6 tbsp of the soaking liquid. Strain this into the cornflour mixture, mix well and set aside. Squeeze out any excess liquid from the mushrooms, remove the tough stalks and slice the caps.

4 Heat the oil in a wok and stir-fry the tofu for 2–3 minutes, until golden. Remove it with a slotted spoon and set aside. Add the mushrooms and the white parts of the spring onions to the wok and stir-fry for 2 minutes. Pour in the cornflour mixture and stir for 1 minute, until thickened. Return the tofu to the wok with the green parts of the spring onions. Simmer for 1–2 minutes. Garnish with basil leaves and serve with noodles.

Stir-fried Chickpeas

Most of the ingredients in this nourishing supper dish come straight from the store cupboard, so it is a useful standby for unexpected guests.

Serves 2–4

30ml/2 tbsp sunflower seeds
400g/14oz can chickpeas, drained and rinsed
5ml/1 tsp chilli powder
5ml/1 tsp paprika
30ml/2 tbsp vegetable oil
1 garlic clove, crushed
200g/7oz can chopped tomatoes
225g/8oz fresh spinach, coarse stalks removed
10ml/2 tsp chilli oil
salt and ground black pepper

1 Heat a wok and then add the sunflower seeds. Dry-fry, stirring frequently, until the seeds are golden and toasted, then tip them into a bowl.

2 Toss the chickpeas in the chilli powder and paprika. Heat the oil in the wok and stir-fry the garlic for 30 seconds. Add the chickpeas and stir-fry for 1 minute.

3 Stir in the tomatoes and stir-fry for 4 minutes. Add the spinach, season well with salt and pepper and toss over the heat for 1 minute.

4 Spoon the stir-fry into a serving dish and drizzle with chilli oil. Sprinkle the sunflower seeds over and serve immediately.

Cook's Tips
• *If you have time, use dried chickpeas, but be prepared to soak them overnight. They are notorious for the time they take to cook, so it is worth making a big batch and either freezing the surplus or using it to make hummus.*
• *Ready-chopped canned tomatoes are usually slightly less watery than canned whole tomatoes, but are more expensive.*
• *Paprika, while never so hot as chilli powder, is available in two forms – mild or sweet and hot.*

Black Bean & Vegetable Stir-fry

The secret of a quick stir-fry is to have everything ready before you begin to cook. This colourful vegetable mixture is coated in a classic Chinese sauce.

Serves 4

8 spring onions (scallions)
225g/8oz/3 cups button (white) mushrooms
1 red (bell) pepper
1 green (bell) pepper
2 large carrots
60ml/4 tbsp sesame oil
2 garlic cloves, crushed
60ml/4 tbsp black bean sauce
90ml/6 tbsp warm water
225g/8oz/2 cups beansprouts
salt and ground black pepper

1 Thinly slice the spring onions and button mushrooms. Cut the red and green peppers in half, remove the seeds and slice the flesh into thin strips.

2 Cut the carrots in half widthways, then cut each half into thin strips lengthways. Stack the slices and cut through them to make very fine strips.

3 Heat the oil in a large wok until it is very hot. Add the spring onions and garlic and stir-fry for 30 seconds.

4 Add the mushrooms, peppers and carrots and stir-fry over a high heat for 5–6 minutes, until the vegetables are just beginning to soften.

5 Mix the black bean sauce with the water. Add to the wok and cook, stirring occasionally, for 3–4 minutes. Stir in the beansprouts and stir-fry for 1 minute more, until all the vegetables are coated in the sauce. Season to taste with salt and pepper. Serve immediately.

Cook's Tip
For best results the oil in the wok must be very hot before adding the vegetables.

Balti Potatoes with Aubergines

Using baby vegetables adds to the attractiveness and the flavour of this dish.

Serves 4

10–12 baby potatoes, unpeeled
15ml/1 tbsp corn oil
2 medium onions, sliced
4–6 curry leaves
2.5ml/ ½ tsp onion seeds
5ml/1 tsp crushed
   coriander seeds
2.5ml/1 tsp cumin seeds
1 medium red (bell) pepper,
   seeded and sliced

5ml/1 tsp grated fresh root ginger
5ml/1 tsp crushed garlic
5ml/1 tsp crushed dried
   red chillies
15ml/1 tbsp chopped
   fresh fenugreek
6 small aubergines (eggplant), cut
   into quarters
5ml/1 tsp chopped fresh
   coriander (cilantro)
15ml/1 tbsp natural (plain)
   low-fat yogurt
fresh coriander (cilantro) leaves,
   to garnish

1 Bring a pan of water to the boil, add the potatoes and cook them for about 20 minutes, until just soft. Drain and set aside.

2 Heat the oil in a wok and cook the onions, curry leaves, onion seeds, crushed coriander seeds and cumin seeds until the onions are a pale golden brown.

3 Add the red pepper strips, ginger, garlic, crushed chillies and fenugreek, followed by the aubergines and potatoes. Stir everything together and cover with a lid. Lower the heat and cook for 5–7 minutes.

4 Remove the lid and add the fresh coriander. Stir in the yogurt. Serve garnished with the coriander leaves.

> **Cook's Tip**
> To prevent curdling it is always best to whisk the yogurt before adding it to a hot dish. If using a larger quantity of yogurt than is required for this recipe, stabilize it with 5ml/1 tsp cornflour (cornstarch) before adding it to a hot dish.

Balti Green Beans with Corn

Frozen green beans are useful for this, as they cook quickly. This dish also makes a colourful accompaniment.

Serves 2

15ml/1 tbsp sunflower oil
1.5ml/ ¼ tsp mustard seeds
1 medium red onion, diced
50g/2oz/ ⅓ cup frozen
   corn kernels
50g/2oz/ ⅓ cup drained canned
   red kidney beans, rinsed

175g/6oz frozen green beans
1 fresh red chilli, seeded
   and diced
1 garlic clove, chopped
2.5cm/1in piece of fresh root
   ginger, finely chopped
15ml/1 tbsp chopped fresh
   coriander (cilantro)
5ml/1 tsp salt
1 tomato, seeded and diced,
   to garnish

1 Heat the oil in a wok. Add the mustard seeds and onion and cook over a low heat, stirring occasionally, for about 2 minutes, until the seeds begin to pop and give off their aroma and the onion is beginning to soften.

2 Add the corn, kidney beans and green beans. Toss over the heat for about 3–5 minutes, until the frozen vegetables have thawed and the beans are crisp-tender.

3 Add the chilli, garlic, ginger, coriander and salt and toss over the heat for 2–3 minutes.

4 Remove the wok from the heat. Transfer the mixture to a warmed serving dish and garnish with the diced tomato.

> **Cook's Tip**
> Strictly speaking, Balti dishes are cooked in a karahi or Balti pan, which is similar to a wok and available in a range of sizes and materials. It is possible to stir-fry in an ordinary frying pan, as long as it is quite deep, but the heat is not distributed so evenly. In Pakistan, the food is often served directly from the karahi, placed on a special stand on the table.

Vegetable Kashmiri

A spicy yogurt sauce coats the vegetables in this aromatic curry.

Serves 4
10ml/2 tsp cumin seeds
8 black peppercorns
seeds from 2 green
   cardamom pods
5cm/2in piece of cinnamon stick
2.5ml/ 1/2 tsp grated nutmeg
45ml/3 tbsp vegetable oil
2.5cm/1in piece of fresh root
   ginger, grated
1 fresh green chilli, chopped
5ml/1 tsp chilli powder
2.5ml/ 1/2 tsp salt
2 large potatoes, cut into chunks
225g/8oz cauliflower, broken
   into florets
225g/8oz okra, thickly sliced
150ml/ 1/4 pint/ 2/3 cup natural
   (plain) yogurt
150ml/ 1/4 pint/ 2/3 cup
   vegetable stock
toasted flaked (sliced) almonds
   and fresh coriander (cilantro)
   sprigs, to garnish

1 Grind the cumin seeds, peppercorns, cardamom seeds, cinnamon stick and nutmeg to a fine powder, using a spice grinder or a mortar and pestle.

2 Heat the oil in a large pan and stir-fry the ginger and fresh chilli for 2 minutes. Add the chilli powder, salt and ground spice mixture and cook for about 2–3 minutes, stirring all the time to prevent the spices from sticking.

3 Stir in the potatoes until coated, cover, and cook over a low heat for 10 minutes, stirring occasionally. Add the cauliflower and okra and cook for 5 minutes.

4 Add the yogurt and stock. Bring to the boil, then lower the heat. Cover and simmer for 20 minutes, or until all the vegetables are tender. Spoon on to a platter, garnish with toasted almonds and coriander sprigs and serve.

> **Cook's Tip**
> An electric coffee grinder will make short work of preparing whole spices. Don't use it for anything else, though.

Masala Okra

Okra or "ladies fingers" are a popular vegetable in India, where they are known as bhindi. In this recipe they are stir-fried with spices.

Serves 4
450g/1lb okra
2.5ml/ 1/2 tsp ground turmeric
5ml/1 tsp mild chilli powder
15ml/1 tbsp ground cumin
15ml/1 tbsp ground coriander
1.5ml/ 1/4 tsp salt
1.5ml/ 1/4 tsp granulated sugar
15ml/1 tbsp lemon juice
15ml/1 tbsp desiccated
   (dry unsweetened
   shredded) coconut
30ml/2 tbsp chopped fresh
   coriander (cilantro)
45ml/3 tbsp vegetable oil
2.5ml/ 1/2 tsp cumin seeds
2.5ml/ 1/2 tsp black
   mustard seeds
chopped fresh tomatoes,
   to garnish
poppadums, to serve

1 Wash, dry and trim the okra. In a bowl, mix together the turmeric, chilli powder, cumin, ground coriander, salt, sugar, lemon juice, desiccated coconut and fresh coriander.

2 Heat the oil in a large, heavy frying pan. Add the cumin and mustard seeds and cook over a low heat, stirring occasionally, for 2 minutes, until they splutter and give off their aroma.

3 Stir in the spice and coconut mixture and cook for 2 minutes more. Add the okra, cover, and cook over a low heat for about 10 minutes, or until tender.

4 Spoon into a serving bowl, garnish with chopped fresh tomatoes and serve with poppadums.

> **Cook's Tips**
> • When buying okra, choose firm, brightly coloured pods that are less than 10cm/4in long. They should snap cleanly. Avoid any that are bendy or browning at the edges or tips.
> • Prepare okra by washing, drying and carefully cutting off the stalk without breaking the seed pod.

Aloo Saag

Potatoes, spinach and spices are the main ingredients in this authentic curried vegetable dish.

Serves 4
450g/1lb fresh young
  spinach leaves
30ml/2 tbsp vegetable oil
5ml/1 tsp black mustard seeds
1 onion, thinly sliced
2 garlic cloves, crushed
2.5cm/1in piece of fresh root
  ginger, finely chopped
675g/1½lb potatoes, cut into
  2.5cm/1in chunks
5ml/1 tsp mild chilli powder
5ml/1 tsp salt
120ml/4fl oz/½ cup water

1 Bring a large pan of lightly salted water to the boil and blanch the spinach leaves for 3–4 minutes. Drain thoroughly and set aside. When the spinach is cool enough to handle, use your hands to squeeze out any remaining liquid.

2 Heat the oil in a large pan. Add the mustard seeds and cook over a low heat, stirring occasionally, for 2 minutes, or until they begin to splutter.

3 Add the onion, garlic and ginger. Cook for 5 minutes, stirring constantly, then add the potatoes, chilli powder, salt and water. Stir well and cook for 8 minutes.

4 Stir in the spinach. Cover and simmer for 10–15 minutes, or until the potatoes are tender. Spoon on to a warmed serving dish and serve immediately.

Cook's Tips
• *Use a waxy variety of potato for this dish, such as Ausonia, Spunta, Maris Bard or Morag, so the pieces do not break up during cooking.*
• *To make certain that the spinach is completely dry after it has been blanched and drained, you can put it in a clean dishtowel, roll up tightly and then squeeze gently to remove the excess liquid.*

Cumin-spiced Marrow & Spinach

Tender chunks of marrow with spinach in a creamy, cumin-flavoured sauce.

Serves 2
½ marrow (large zucchini), about
  450g/1lb
30ml/2 tbsp vegetable oil
10ml/2 tsp cumin seeds
1 small fresh red chilli, seeded
  and finely chopped
30ml/2 tbsp water
50g/2oz fresh young spinach
  leaves, torn into pieces
90ml/6 tbsp single (light) cream
salt and ground black pepper
boiled rice or naan bread,
  to serve

1 Peel the marrow with a vegetable peeler and cut it in half. Using a spoon, scoop out and discard the seeds. Cut the flesh into cubes.

2 Heat the oil in a large, heavy frying pan. Add the cumin seeds and the chopped chilli. Cook over a low heat, stirring occasionally, for 1 minute.

3 Add the marrow and measured water to the pan. Cover with foil or a lid and simmer gently, stirring occasionally, for about 8 minutes, until the marrow is just tender. Remove the foil cover or lid and cook for about 2 minutes more, or until most of the water has evaporated.

4 Add the spinach to the marrow, with just the water that clings to the leaves after washing and draining. Replace the cover and cook gently for 1 minute.

5 Stir in the cream and cook over a high heat for 2 minutes, but do not allow the mixture to boil. Season to taste with salt and pepper and serve with rice or naan bread.

Cook's Tip
Be careful when handling chillies, as the juice can burn sensitive skin. Wear rubber gloves to protect your hands or wash your hands very thoroughly after preparation.

Mushroom & Okra Curry

This simple but delicious curry is served with a fresh gingery mango relish.

Serves 4

4 garlic cloves, coarsely chopped
2.5cm/1in piece of fresh root
   ginger, coarsely chopped
1–2 fresh red chillies, seeded
   and chopped
175ml/6fl oz/ ³⁄₄ cup cold water
15ml/1 tbsp sunflower oil
5ml/1 tsp coriander seeds
5ml/1 tsp cumin seeds
5ml/1 tsp ground cumin
seeds from 2 green cardamom
   pods, ground
pinch of ground turmeric
400g/14oz can
   chopped tomatoes

450g/1lb/6 cups mushrooms,
   quartered if large
225g/8oz okra, trimmed and cut
   into 1cm/ ¹⁄₂in slices
30ml/2 tbsp chopped fresh
   coriander (cilantro)
cooked basmati rice,
   to serve

For the mango relish

1 large ripe mango, about
   500g/1¹⁄₄lb
1 small garlic clove, crushed
1 onion, finely chopped
10ml/2 tsp grated fresh
   root ginger
1 fresh red chilli, seeded and
   finely chopped
pinch of granulated sugar
pinch of salt

1 First, make the relish. Peel the mango and cut the flesh from either side of the stone (pit). Mash it in a bowl or pulse it in a food processor. Stir in the remaining relish ingredients. Set aside.

2 Put the garlic, ginger, chillies and 45ml/3 tbsp of the water into a blender and process until smooth.

3 Heat the oil in a large pan. Add the coriander and cumin seeds and let them sizzle for a few seconds. Add the ground cumin, cardamom and turmeric and cook for 1 minute. Add the paste from the blender, the tomatoes, the remaining water, the mushrooms and okra. Stir and bring to the boil. Lower the heat, cover and simmer for 5 minutes.

4 Uncover and cook for 10 minutes more, until the okra is tender. Stir in the chopped coriander and serve immediately with the mango relish and rice.

Bengali-style Vegetables

Many curries need to be cooked slowly if their full flavour is to be realized. This one is very quick and easy, thanks to spices that rapidly release their properties.

Serves 4

¹⁄₂ cauliflower, broken into florets
1 large potato, peeled and cut
   into 2.5cm/1in dice
115g/4oz green beans, trimmed
2 courgettes (zucchini), halved
   lengthways and sliced
2 fresh green chillies, seeded
   and chopped

2.5cm/1in piece of fresh root
   ginger, finely chopped
120ml/4fl oz/ ¹⁄₂ cup natural
   (plain) yogurt
10ml/2 tsp ground coriander
2.5ml/ ¹⁄₂ tsp ground turmeric
25g/1oz/2 tbsp ghee or
   clarified butter
2.5ml/ ¹⁄₂ tsp garam masala
5ml/1 tsp cumin seeds
10ml/2 tsp granulated sugar
pinch of ground cloves
pinch of ground cinnamon
pinch of ground cardamom
salt and ground black pepper

1 Bring a large pan of lightly salted water to the boil. Add the cauliflower and potato and cook for 5 minutes. Add the beans and courgettes and cook for 2–3 minutes more.

2 Drain the vegetables and tip them into a bowl. Add the chillies, ginger, yogurt, ground coriander and turmeric. Season with plenty of salt and pepper and mix well.

3 Heat the ghee in a large frying pan. Add the vegetable mixture and cook over a high heat for 2 minutes, stirring.

4 Stir in the garam masala and whole cumin seeds and cook for 2 minutes. Stir in the sugar and the remaining spices. Cook for about 1 minute, or until all the liquid has evaporated. Serve.

Cook's Tip
To clarify butter, melt 50g/2oz/ ¹⁄₄ cup butter in a small pan. Remove from the heat and leave for 5 minutes. Pour off the clear yellow clarified butter, leaving the sediment in the pan.

Spinach with Mushrooms & Red Pepper

This is a wonderful way to cook three tasty and nutritious vegetables. Serve the stir-fry very hot, with freshly made chapatis.

Serves 4
450g/1lb fresh or frozen spinach
30ml/2 tbsp corn oil
2 onions, diced
6–8 curry leaves
1.5ml/ ¼ tsp onion seeds
5ml/1 tsp crushed garlic
5ml/1 tsp grated fresh root ginger
5ml/1 tsp mild chilli powder
5ml/1 tsp salt
7.5ml/1 ½ tsp ground coriander
1 large red (bell) pepper, seeded and sliced
115g/4oz/1 ½ cups mushrooms, coarsely chopped
225g/8oz/1 cup low-fat fromage frais or 250ml/8fl oz/1 cup low-fat natural (plain) yogurt
30ml/2 tbsp fresh coriander (cilantro) leaves

1 Blanch fresh spinach briefly in boiling water and drain thoroughly. Thaw frozen spinach, then drain. Set aside.

2 Heat the oil in a wok. Add the onions, curry leaves and onion seeds and cook, stirring occasionally, for 1–2 minutes. Add the garlic, ginger, chilli powder, salt and ground coriander. Stir-fry for 2–3 minutes more.

3 Add half the red pepper slices and all the mushrooms and continue to stir-fry for 2–3 minutes.

4 Add the spinach and stir-fry for 4–6 minutes. Finally, stir in the fromage frais or yogurt and half the fresh coriander, followed by the remaining red pepper slices. Cook over a medium heat, stirring constantly, for 2–3 minutes more before serving, garnished with the remaining coriander.

Variation
For a spicier dish, add one finely chopped fresh red chilli with the (bell) pepper slices in step 3.

Rice Noodles with Vegetable Chilli Sauce

A mixture of fresh and canned ingredients, this is a very versatile dish.

Serves 4
15ml/1 tbsp sunflower oil
1 onion, chopped
2 garlic cloves, crushed
1 fresh red chilli, seeded and finely chopped
1 red (bell) pepper, seeded and diced
2 carrots, finely chopped
175g/6oz/1 ½ cups baby corn cobs, halved
225g/8oz can sliced bamboo shoots, drained and rinsed
400g/14oz can red kidney beans, drained and rinsed
300ml/ ½ pint/1 ¼ cups passata (bottled strained tomatoes) or sieved tomatoes
15ml/1 tbsp soy sauce
5ml/1 tsp ground coriander
250g/9oz rice noodles
30ml/2 tbsp chopped fresh coriander (cilantro)
salt and ground black pepper
fresh parsley sprigs, to garnish

1 Heat the oil in a large pan and cook the onion, garlic, chilli and red pepper, stirring occasionally, for 5 minutes. Stir in the carrots, corn, bamboo shoots, kidney beans, passata or sieved tomatoes, soy sauce and ground coriander. Bring to the boil, then lower the heat, cover and simmer, stirring occasionally, for 30 minutes, until the vegetables are tender. Season to taste.

2 Meanwhile, bring a large pan of water to the boil, add the noodles and remove the pan from the heat. Cover and leave to stand for about 4 minutes, until the noodles are just tender. Drain thoroughly, rinse with boiling water and drain again.

3 Stir the coriander into the sauce. Spoon the noodles into bowls, top with the sauce, garnish with parsley and serve.

Cook's Tip
Rice noodles are specified here, but you can use any type of noodles or even spaghetti.

Balti Mushrooms in a Creamy Garlic Sauce

Low-fat and virtually fat-free fromage frais are real finds for anyone who is trying to limit the amount of fat he or she consumes. It gives this stir-fry a deceptively creamy taste.

Serves 4
15ml/1 tbsp olive oil
1 bay leaf
3 garlic cloves, coarsely chopped
2 fresh green chillies, seeded and chopped
350g/12oz/4½ cups button (white) mushrooms, halved
30–45ml/2–3 tbsp vegetable stock
225g/8oz/1 cup low-fat fromage frais or 250ml/8fl oz/1 cup low-fat natural (plain) yogurt
15ml/1 tbsp chopped fresh mint
15ml/1 tbsp chopped fresh coriander (cilantro)
5ml/1 tsp salt
fresh mint and coriander (cilantro) leaves, to garnish

1 Heat the oil in a wok, add the bay leaf, garlic and chillies and cook for about 1 minute.

2 Add the mushrooms and moisten them with the stock. Cook over a high heat, stirring constantly, for 3–5 minutes, until the stock has been absorbed.

3 Remove the wok from the heat and stir in the fromage frais or yogurt, mint, chopped coriander and salt. Return the wok to the heat and cook, stirring constantly, for 2 minutes, until heated through. Transfer to a warmed serving dish. Garnish with the mint and coriander leaves and serve immediately.

Cook's Tip
All kinds of mushrooms will absorb an astonishing amount of fat, as anyone who has cooked them in butter or oil will appreciate. Try using a well-flavoured, home-made vegetable stock instead; the mushrooms will cook beautifully and will remain lovely and juicy.

Corn & Cauliflower Balti

This quick and tasty vegetable dish is easily made with frozen corn.

Serves 4
15ml/1 tbsp corn oil
4 curry leaves
1.5ml/¼ tsp onion seeds
2 medium onions, diced
1 fresh red chilli, seeded and diced
175g/6oz/1 cup frozen corn kernels
½ small cauliflower, cut into small florets
6 fresh mint leaves

1 Heat the oil in a wok. Add the curry leaves and the onion seeds and stir-fry for about 30 seconds.

2 Add the onions and stir-fry for 5–8 minutes, until golden brown. Stir in the chilli, corn and cauliflower and stir-fry for 5–8 minutes.

3 Finally, add the mint leaves and serve immediately.

Glazed Mangetouts & Peppers

A delectable sauce coats the crisp-tender vegetables in this simple stir-fry.

Serves 2–4
5ml/1 tsp cornflour (cornstarch)
10ml/2 tsp dry sherry
15ml/1 tbsp soy sauce
90ml/6 tbsp vegetable stock
15ml/1 tbsp sweet chilli sauce
15ml/1 tbsp sunflower oil
2 red (bell) peppers, seeded and sliced
115g/4oz/1 cup mangetouts (snow peas)

1 Mix the cornflour to a paste with the sherry. Stir in the soy sauce, stock and chilli sauce.
2 Heat the oil in a wok and stir-fry the pepper slices and mangetouts for 2–3 minutes, until crisp-tender.
3 Stir in the cornflour mixture and toss over the heat for 1–2 minutes, until the vegetables are glistening and the sauce is hot. Serve immediately.

Tagliatelle with Pea Sauce, Asparagus & Broad Beans

A creamy pea sauce provides a wonderful contrast to the crunchy young vegetables.

Serves 4

15ml/1 tbsp olive oil
1 garlic clove, crushed
6 spring onions (scallions), sliced
225g/8oz/2 cups frozen peas, thawed
30ml/2 tbsp chopped fresh sage, plus extra leaves to garnish
finely grated rind of 2 lemons
450ml/¾ pint/scant 2 cups vegetable stock
350g/12oz fresh young asparagus, trimmed and cut into 5cm/2in lengths
225g/8oz/2 cups frozen broad (fava) beans, thawed
450g/1lb/2 cups fresh or dried tagliatelle
60ml/4 tbsp low-fat natural (plain) yogurt, whisked

1 Heat the oil in a pan. Add the garlic and spring onions and cook over a low heat, stirring occasionally, for 2–3 minutes, until softened, but not coloured.

2 Add the peas, sage, lemon rind and stock. Stir in one-third of the asparagus stalks. Bring to the boil, lower the heat and simmer for 10 minutes, until tender. Process in a blender until smooth, then scrape into a pan.

3 Pop the broad beans out of their skins and set them aside. Bring a large pan of water to the boil, add the remaining asparagus and blanch for 2 minutes. Transfer the asparagus pieces to a colander with a slotted spoon and set aside.

4 Bring the water in the pan back to the boil, add the tagliatelle and cook for about 10 minutes, until it is *al dente*.

5 Meanwhile, add the cooked asparagus and shelled beans to the sauce and reheat. Remove the pan from the heat and stir the yogurt into the sauce. Drain the pasta and divide among four warmed plates. Top the pasta with the sauce. Garnish with a few extra sage leaves and serve immediately.

Mushroom Bolognese

A quick – and exceedingly tasty – vegetarian version of the classic Italian meat dish.

Serves 4

15ml/1 tbsp olive oil
1 onion, chopped
1 garlic clove, crushed
450g/1lb/6 cups mushrooms, quartered
15ml/1 tbsp tomato purée (paste)
400g/14oz can chopped tomatoes
15ml/1 tbsp chopped fresh oregano
450g/1lb fresh pasta
salt and ground black pepper
chopped fresh oregano, to garnish
Parmesan cheese, to serve

1 Heat the oil in a large pan. Add the chopped onion and garlic and cook over a low heat, stirring occasionally, for 2–3 minutes, until just beginning to soften.

2 Add the mushrooms to the pan and cook over a high heat, stirring occasionally, for 3–4 minutes.

3 Stir in the tomato purée, chopped tomatoes and oregano. Lower the heat, cover and cook for 5 minutes.

4 Meanwhile, bring a large pan of lightly salted water to the boil. Cook the pasta for 2–3 minutes until *al dente*.

5 Season the mushroom sauce to taste with salt and pepper. Drain the pasta, tip it into a bowl and add the mushroom mixture. Toss thoroughly to mix. Serve in warmed, individual bowls. Add a sprinkling of extra oregano and top with shavings of fresh Parmesan cheese.

Cook's Tips
• *If you prefer to use dried pasta, make it the first thing that you cook. It will take 10–12 minutes, during which time you can make the mushroom sauce.*
• *This dish is even more delicious if you use wild mushrooms, such as ceps, oysters and chanterelles.*

Five-spice Vegetable Noodles

Vary this stir-fry by substituting mushrooms, bamboo shoots, beansprouts, mangetouts or water chestnuts for some or all of the vegetables.

Serves 2–3
225g/8oz dried egg noodles
30ml/2 tbsp sesame oil
2 carrots
1 celery stick
1 small fennel bulb
2 courgettes (zucchini), halved lengthways and sliced
1 fresh red chilli
2.5cm/1in piece of fresh root ginger, grated
1 garlic clove, crushed
7.5ml/1½ tsp Chinese five-spice powder
2.5ml/½ tsp ground cinnamon
4 spring onions (scallions), sliced
60ml/4 tbsp warm water

1 Bring a large pan of salted water to the boil. Add the noodles and cook for 2–3 minutes, until they are just tender. Drain the noodles, return them to the pan and toss them with a little of the oil. Set aside.

2 Cut the carrots and celery into small, thin strips. Cut the fennel bulb in half and cut out the hard core. Cut into slices, then cut the slices into small, thin strips.

3 Heat the remaining oil in a wok until very hot. Add the carrots, celery, fennel and courgettes and stir-fry over a medium heat for 7–8 minutes.

4 Cut half the chilli into rings, discarding any seeds, and set aside. Chop the rest of the chilli and add it to the wok.

5 Add the ginger and garlic and stir-fry for 2 minutes, then add the Chinese five-spice powder and cinnamon. Stir-fry for 1 minute, then toss in the spring onions and stir-fry for a further minute.

6 Pour in the warm water and cook for 1 minute. Stir in the noodles and toss over the heat until they have warmed through. Transfer to a warmed serving dish and serve sprinkled with the reserved sliced red chilli.

Fried Noodles with Beansprouts & Asparagus

Soft fried noodles contrast beautifully with crisp beansprouts and asparagus.

Serves 2
115g/4oz dried egg noodles
45ml/3 tbsp vegetable oil
1 small onion, chopped
2.5cm/1in piece of fresh root ginger, grated
2 garlic cloves, crushed
175g/6oz young asparagus spears, trimmed
115g/4oz/1 cup beansprouts
4 spring onions (scallions), sliced
45ml/3 tbsp soy sauce
salt and ground black pepper

1 Bring a pan of lightly salted water to the boil. Add the noodles and cook for 2–3 minutes, until just tender. Drain and toss with 15ml/1 tbsp of the oil.

2 Heat the remaining oil in a wok until very hot. Add the onion, ginger and garlic and stir-fry for 2–3 minutes. Add the asparagus and stir-fry for 2–3 minutes more.

3 Add the noodles and beansprouts and toss over a high heat for 2 minutes.

4 Stir in the spring onions and soy sauce. Season to taste with salt and pepper. Stir-fry for 1 minute, then serve.

Cook's Tip
When seasoning the stir-fry, add salt sparingly, as the soy sauce will impart quite a salty flavour.

Variation
If you like, substitute the same quantity of mangetouts (snow peas) for the asparagus spears.

Soufflé Omelette with Mushrooms

A soufflé omelette makes an ideal meal for one, especially with this delicious filling. Use a combination of different mushrooms, such as oyster and chestnut, if you like.

Serves 1

2 eggs, separated
15ml/1 tbsp water
15g/½oz/1 tbsp butter
fresh flat leaf parsley or coriander (cilantro) leaves, to garnish

For the mushroom sauce
15g/½ oz/1 tbsp butter
75g/3oz/generous 1 cup button (white) mushrooms, thinly sliced
15ml/1 tbsp plain (all-purpose) flour
90–120ml/3–4fl oz/⅓–½ cup milk
5ml/1 tsp chopped fresh parsley (optional)
salt and ground black pepper

1 Start by making the mushroom sauce. Melt the butter in a pan over a low heat. Add the sliced mushrooms and cook gently, stirring occasionally, for 4–5 minutes, until tender.

2 Stir in the flour and cook, stirring constantly, for 1 minute, then gradually add the milk, stirring constantly until the sauce boils and thickens. Add the parsley, if using, and season to taste with salt and pepper. Keep the sauce hot while you are making the omelette.

3 Beat the egg yolks with the water and season with salt and pepper. Whisk the egg whites until stiff, then fold them into the egg yolks, using a metal spoon. Preheat the grill (broiler).

4 Melt the butter in a large, heavy frying pan which can safely be used under the grill. (Cover a wooden handle with foil to protect it.) Pour in the egg mixture. Cook over a gentle heat for 2–4 minutes, then place the frying pan under the grill and cook for 3–4 minutes more, until the top of the omelette is golden brown.

5 Slide the omelette on to a warmed serving plate, pour the mushroom sauce over the top and fold the omelette in half. Garnish with parsley or coriander leaves and serve.

Coriander Omelette Parcels with Asian Vegetables

Stir-fried vegetables in black bean sauce make a remarkably good omelette filling, which is quick and easy to prepare.

Serves 4

130g/4½ oz broccoli, cut into small florets
30ml/2 tbsp groundnut (peanut) oil
1cm/½in piece of fresh root ginger, finely grated
1 large garlic clove, crushed
2 fresh red chillies, seeded and thinly sliced
4 spring onions (scallions), sliced diagonally
175g/6oz/3 cups shredded pak choi (bok choy)
50g/2oz/2 cups fresh coriander (cilantro) leaves, plus extra to garnish
115g/4oz/1 cup beansprouts
45ml/3 tbsp black bean sauce
4 eggs
salt and ground black pepper

1 Bring a large pan of lightly salted water to the boil, add the broccoli and blanch for 2 minutes. Drain, refresh under cold running water, then drain again.

2 Heat half the oil in a wok and stir-fry the ginger, garlic and half the chillies for 1 minute. Add the spring onions, broccoli and pak choi and stir-fry for 2 minutes more. Chop three-quarters of the coriander leaves and add to the wok with the beansprouts. Stir-fry for 1 minute, then add the black bean sauce and toss over the heat for 1 minute more. Remove the pan from the heat and keep the vegetables hot.

3 Beat the eggs and season. Heat a little of the remaining oil in a small frying pan and add one-quarter of the beaten egg. Swirl to cover the base, then sprinkle over one-quarter of the whole coriander leaves. Cook the omelette until set, then turn it out on to a plate. Make three more, adding more oil as required.

4 Divide the stir-fry among the omelettes and roll them up. Cut each one in half crossways and arrange the pieces on a plate. Garnish with coriander leaves and the remaining chillies.

MIDWEEK MEALS

This chapter is full of inspiring recipes that are easy to make, packed with flavour and bursting with goodness to add variety and interest to everyday meals. And variety is the keynote with a fabulous collection of tasty dishes from countries around the world – from India to Mexico. If you thought rice was just rice, think again. In the Middle East, it is delicately flavoured with aromatic spices and combined with nuts, dried fruit and pulses, while in Italy it is cooked to a uniquely creamy consistency with vegetables, mushrooms and fresh herbs. Pilaffs and risottos are both delicious, but have nothing more in common than their basic ingredient. Beans and pulses, those reliable mainstays of the vegetarian diet, are infinitely versatile. You simply can't compare the hearty richness of Jamaican Black Bean Pot with the subtle spiciness of Moroccan Aubergine & Chickpea Tagine – but you can certainly relish both of them.

This chapter also includes some imaginative variations of perennially popular recipes. Mixed Vegetable & Macaroni Gratin elevates humble macaroni cheese to new culinary heights, while Spring Vegetable Omelette works a similar magic on the rather unexciting Spanish potato tortilla. You may be pleasantly surprised by the choice of tasty pasta sauces, which range from light and summery to substantial and spicy, and you probably didn't know that pizzas can be healthy food, too.

Finally, all the recipes in this chapter are practical choices for midweek meals. They are all easy to prepare with readily available ingredients. Some take only a short time to cook and can be on the table within half an hour. Others can be assembled, popped in the oven and left to their own devices, giving you a well-earned chance to unwind and catch up with the family news.

Spaghetti with Fresh Tomato Sauce

This famous Neapolitan sauce is very simple, so nothing detracts from the rich, sweet flavour of the tomatoes themselves.

Serves 4
675g/1½ lb ripe Italian plum tomatoes
60ml/4 tbsp olive oil
1 onion, finely chopped
350g/12oz fresh or dried spaghetti
a small handful of fresh basil leaves, shredded
salt and ground black pepper
coarsely shaved Parmesan cheese, to serve

1 Cut a cross in the blossom end of each tomato and put them in a heatproof bowl. Pour over boiling water to cover and leave for about 30 seconds, or until the skins wrinkle and start to peel back from the crosses. Drain, peel off the skin and coarsely chop the flesh.

2 Heat the oil in a large pan and cook the onion over a low heat, stirring occasionally, for 5 minutes, until softened and lightly coloured. Stir in the tomatoes and season to taste with salt and pepper. Cover the pan and cook over a low heat, stirring occasionally for 30–40 minutes.

3 Bring a large pan of lightly salted water to the boil and cook the spaghetti until it is al dente. Dried pasta will take about 12 minutes and fresh spaghetti about 3–4 minutes.

4 Remove the sauce from the heat and taste for seasoning. Drain the pasta, tip it into a warmed bowl, pour the sauce over and toss well. Sprinkle the fresh basil over the top and serve immediately, with shaved Parmesan handed separately.

Cook's Tip
In summer, when sun-ripened tomatoes are plentiful, make this sauce in bulk and freeze it for later use. Let it cool, then freeze in usable quantities in rigid containers. Thaw before reheating.

Penne Rigate with Green Vegetable Sauce

Strictly speaking, this isn't a sauced dish, but a medley of vegetables and pasta tossed in butter and oil.

Serves 4
25g/1oz/2 tbsp butter
45ml/3 tbsp extra virgin olive oil
1 small leek, thinly sliced
2 carrots, diced
2.5ml/ ½ tsp granulated sugar
1 courgette (zucchini), diced
75g/3oz green beans, cut into short lengths
115g/4oz/1 cup frozen peas
450g/1lb/4 cups dried penne rigate or other pasta shapes
a handful of fresh flat leaf parsley, chopped, plus extra, deep-fried, to garnish
2 ripe Italian plum tomatoes, peeled and diced
salt and ground black pepper

1 Melt the butter in the oil in a pan. When the mixture sizzles, add the leek and carrots. Sprinkle the sugar over and cook, stirring frequently, for about 5 minutes.

2 Stir in the courgette, green beans and peas and season with salt and pepper. Cover and cook over a low heat, stirring occasionally, for 10 minutes, or until the vegetables are tender.

3 Meanwhile, bring a large pan of lightly salted water to the boil and cook the pasta until it is al dente.

4 Drain the pasta and return it to the pan. Stir the parsley and tomatoes into the sauce and season. Pour the sauce over the pasta, toss to mix, then serve with the deep-fried parsley.

Variation
For a quick and easy baked dish, make the vegetable mixture without the tomatoes. Toss it with the pasta and spoon it into an ovenproof dish. Slice three tomatoes and arrange them over the vegetable mixture. Top with a thick layer of grated cheese, then grill (broil) until the cheese melts.

Rigatoni with Winter Tomato Sauce

In winter, when fresh tomatoes are not at their best, Italians use canned tomatoes to make this superb sauce, which is particularly good with chunky pasta shapes.

Serves 6–8
30ml/2 tbsp olive oil
1 garlic clove, thinly sliced
1 onion, finely chopped
1 carrot, finely chopped
1 celery stick, finely chopped
a few leaves each fresh
  basil, thyme and oregano
  or marjoram
2 x 400g/14oz cans chopped
  Italian plum tomatoes
15ml/1 tbsp sun-dried
  tomato paste
5ml/1 tsp granulated sugar
about 90ml/6 tbsp dry red or
  white wine (optional)
350g/12oz/3 cups dried rigatoni
salt and ground black pepper
chopped fresh mixed herbs,
  such as thyme and basil, to
  garnish (optional)
coarsely shaved Parmesan
  cheese, to serve

1 Heat the olive oil in a medium pan, add the garlic slices and cook over a very low heat, stirring constantly, for 1–2 minutes.

2 Add the onion, carrot, celery, basil, thyme and oregano or marjoram. Cook over a low heat, stirring frequently, for 5–7 minutes, until all the vegetables have softened and are lightly coloured.

3 Add the canned tomatoes, tomato paste and sugar, then stir in the wine, if using. Season with salt and pepper to taste. Bring to the boil, stirring constantly, then lower the heat and simmer for about 45 minutes, stirring occasionally.

4 Meanwhile, bring a large pan of lightly salted water to the boil and cook the pasta for 12 minutes or until *al dente*. Drain it and tip it into a warmed bowl.

5 Pour the sauce over the rigatoni and toss well. If you like, garnish with extra chopped herbs. Serve immediately, with shavings of Parmesan handed separately.

Whole-wheat Pasta with Caraway Cabbage

Crunchy cabbage and Brussels sprouts are the perfect partners for pasta in this healthy dish.

Serves 6
30ml/2 tbsp olive oil
3 onions, coarsely chopped
400ml/14fl oz/1⅔ cups
  vegetable stock
350g/12oz round white cabbage,
  coarsely chopped
350g/12oz Brussels sprouts,
  trimmed and halved
10ml/2 tsp caraway seeds
15ml/1 tbsp chopped fresh dill
200g/7oz/1¾ cups fresh or dried
  whole-wheat pasta spirals
salt and ground black pepper
fresh dill sprigs, to garnish

1 Heat the oil in a large pan. Add the onions and cook over a low heat, stirring occasionally, for 10 minutes, until softened and golden in colour. If they start to stick to the pan, moisten them with a little of the stock.

2 Add the chopped cabbage and Brussels sprouts and cook for 2–3 minutes, then stir in the caraway seeds and chopped dill. Pour in the remaining stock and season with salt and pepper to taste. Cover and simmer for 5–10 minutes, until the cabbage and sprouts are crisp-tender.

3 Meanwhile, bring a pan of lightly salted water to the boil and cook the pasta for 12 minutes, or until *al dente*.

4 Drain the pasta, tip it into a warmed bowl and add the cabbage mixture. Toss lightly, adjust the seasoning, if necessary, and serve immediately, garnished with dill.

Cook's Tips
• If tiny baby Brussels sprouts are available, they can be used whole for this dish.
• Not only do caraway seeds complement the flavour of cabbage, they also make it more digestible.

Pasta with Spicy Aubergine Sauce

There's no better way to satisfy hearty appetites than with a big bowl of pasta in a rich and robust sauce.

Serves 4–6
30ml/2 tbsp olive oil
1 small fresh red chilli
2 garlic cloves
2 handfuls of fresh flat leaf
    parsley, coarsely chopped
450g/1lb aubergines (eggplant),
    coarsely chopped
1 handful of fresh basil leaves
200ml/7fl oz/scant 1 cup water
1 vegetable stock (bouillon) cube
8 ripe Italian plum tomatoes,
    peeled and finely chopped
60ml/4 tbsp red wine
5ml/1 tsp granulated sugar
1 sachet saffron powder
2.5ml/ ½ tsp ground paprika
350g/12oz/3 cups dried
    pasta shapes
salt and ground black pepper
chopped fresh herbs,
    to garnish

1 Heat the oil in a large pan and add the chilli, garlic cloves and half the chopped parsley. Smash the garlic cloves with a wooden spoon to release their juices, then cover the pan and cook over a low heat, stirring occasionally, for about 10 minutes.

2 Remove and discard the chilli. Add the aubergines to the pan with the rest of the parsley and all the basil. Pour in half the water. Crumble in the stock cube and stir until it has dissolved, then cover and cook, stirring frequently, for about 10 minutes.

3 Add the tomatoes, wine, sugar, saffron and paprika, season with salt and pepper, then pour in the remaining water. Stir well, replace the lid and cook, stirring occasionally, for 30–40 minutes.

4 Meanwhile, bring a pan of lightly salted water to the boil. Cook the pasta for about 12 minutes, until *al dente*. Drain, tip into a bowl and toss with the sauce. Garnish with fresh herbs.

> **Variation**
> *This sauce can be layered with sheets of pasta and béchamel or cheese sauce to make a delicious vegetarian lasagne.*

Pasta with Sugocasa & Chilli

This is a quick version of a popular Italian dish, *pasta arrabbiata*. The name literally translates as "furious pasta", a reference to the heat generated by the chilli.

Serves 4
475ml/16fl oz/2 cups bottled
    sugocasa (see Cook's Tip)
2 garlic cloves, crushed
150ml/ ¼ pint/ ⅔ cup dry
    white wine
15ml/1 tbsp sun-dried
    tomato paste
1 fresh red chilli
300g/11oz/2¾ cups dried penne
    or other pasta shapes
60ml/4 tbsp finely chopped fresh
    flat leaf parsley
salt and ground black pepper
freshly grated pecorino cheese,
    to serve

1 Put the sugocasa, garlic, wine, sun-dried tomato paste and chilli in a pan and bring to the boil. Lower the heat, cover and simmer for about 15 minutes, until thick.

2 Meanwhile, bring a large pan of lightly salted water to the boil. Add the pasta shapes and cook for 10–12 minutes, until they are *al dente*.

3 Using tongs, remove the chilli from the sauce. Taste for seasoning. If you prefer a hotter taste, chop some or all of the chilli and return it to the sauce.

4 Drain the pasta and tip it into a large bowl. Stir half the parsley into the sauce, then pour the sauce over the pasta and toss to mix. Serve immediately, sprinkled with grated pecorino and the remaining parsley.

> **Cook's Tip**
> *Sugocasa is sold in bottles and is sometimes labelled "crushed Italian tomatoes". It is finer than canned chopped tomatoes and coarser than passata (bottled strained tomatoes), and so is ideal for pasta sauces, soups and stews.*

Mixed Vegetable & Macaroni Gratin

A tasty change from macaroni cheese, this dish is great for a family meal.

Serves 6

225g/8oz/2 cups
  whole-wheat macaroni
450ml/³⁄₄ cup/scant 2 cups
  vegetable stock
225g/8oz leeks, sliced
225g/8oz broccoli florets
50g/2oz/4 tbsp half-fat spread
50g/2oz/ ¹⁄₂ cup wholemeal
  (whole-wheat) flour

600ml/1 pint/2¹⁄₂ cups
  skimmed milk
115g/4oz/1 cup grated mature
  (sharp) Cheddar cheese
5ml/1 tsp prepared English
  (hot) mustard
350g/12oz can corn
  kernels, drained
25g/1oz/ ¹⁄₂ cup fresh wholemeal
  (whole-wheat) breadcrumbs
30ml/2 tbsp chopped
  fresh parsley
2 tomatoes, cut into eighths
salt and ground black pepper

1 Preheat the oven to 200°C/400°F/Gas 6. Bring a large pan of lightly salted water to the boil and cook the macaroni for 8–10 minutes, until *al dente*.

2 Meanwhile, heat the stock in a separate pan and cook the leeks for 8 minutes. Add the broccoli florets and cook for 2 minutes more. Drain, reserving 300ml/½ pint/1¼ cups of the vegetable stock.

3 Put the half-fat spread, flour and milk in a pan. Add the reserved stock. Heat gently, whisking constantly, until the sauce comes to the boil and has thickened slightly. Simmer gently for 3 minutes, stirring constantly.

4 Remove the pan from the heat, stir in two-thirds of the cheese, then add the macaroni, leeks, broccoli, mustard and corn. Mix well and season with salt and pepper to taste. Transfer the mixture to an ovenproof dish.

5 Mix the remaining cheese, breadcrumbs and parsley and sprinkle the mixture over the surface. Arrange the tomatoes on top and then bake for 30–40 minutes, until the topping is golden brown and bubbling.

Spinach & Hazelnut Lasagne

Using low-fat fromage frais or yogurt instead of a white sauce makes this a healthy version of a popular dish.

Serves 4

900g/2lb fresh spinach
300ml/ ¹⁄₂ pint/1¹⁄₄ cups
  vegetable stock
1 medium onion, finely chopped
1 garlic clove, crushed
75g/3oz/ ³⁄₄ cup hazelnuts

30ml/2 tbsp chopped fresh basil
6 sheets no pre-cook lasagne
400g/14oz can
  chopped tomatoes
200g/7oz/scant 1 cup low-fat
  fromage frais or 200ml/
  7fl oz/scant 1 cup low-fat
  natural (plain) yogurt
salt and ground black pepper
flaked (sliced) hazelnuts and
  chopped fresh parsley,
  to garnish

1 Preheat the oven to 200°C/400°F/Gas 6. Wash the spinach and place it in a pan with just the water that is still clinging to the leaves. Cover and cook over a fairly high heat for about 2 minutes, until the spinach has wilted. Drain well and set aside until required.

2 Heat 30ml/2 tbsp of the stock in a large pan. Add the onion and garlic, bring to the boil, then simmer until softened. Stir in the spinach, hazelnuts and basil.

3 In a large ovenproof dish, make layers of the spinach, lasagne and tomatoes. Season each layer with salt and pepper to taste. Pour over the remaining stock. Spread the fromage frais or yogurt evenly over the top.

4 Bake the lasagne for about 45 minutes, or until golden brown. Serve hot, garnished with lines of flaked hazelnuts and chopped fresh parsley.

Cook's Tip
The flavour of hazelnuts is improved if they are roasted. Place them on a baking sheet and bake in a moderate oven or under a hot grill (broiler) until light golden.

Courgette, Corn & Plum Tomato Whole-wheat Pizza

This flavoursome pizza has a colourful topping. It is good hot or cold.

Serves 6

225g/8oz/2 cups wholemeal (whole-wheat) flour
pinch of salt
10ml/2 tsp baking powder
50g/2oz/4 tbsp margarine
150ml/ ¼ pint/ ⅔ cup skimmed milk
30ml/2 tbsp tomato purée (paste)
10ml/2 tsp dried herbes de Provence

10ml/2 tsp olive oil
1 onion, sliced
1 garlic clove, crushed
2 small courgettes (zucchini), sliced
115g/4oz/1 ½ cups mushrooms, sliced
115g/4oz/ ⅔ cup frozen corn kernels
2 plum tomatoes, sliced
50g/2oz/ ½ cup grated reduced-fat Red Leicester cheese
50g/2oz/ ½ cup grated half-fat mozzarella cheese
salt and ground black pepper
fresh basil sprigs, to garnish

1 Preheat the oven to 220°C/425°F/Gas 7. Line a baking sheet with non-stick baking parchment. Put the flour, salt and baking powder in a bowl and rub in the margarine until the mixture resembles breadcrumbs. Add enough milk to form a soft dough and knead lightly. Roll the dough out on a lightly floured surface, to a round about 25cm/10in in diameter.

2 Place the dough on the prepared baking sheet and pinch the edges to make a rim. Spread the tomato purée over the base and sprinkle the herbs on top.

3 Heat the oil in a frying pan and cook the onion, garlic, courgettes and mushrooms gently for 10 minutes, stirring occasionally. Spread the vegetable mixture over the pizza base, sprinkle over the corn and season to taste with salt and pepper. Arrange the tomato slices on top. Mix the cheeses and sprinkle over the pizza. Bake for 25–30 minutes, until cooked and golden brown. Serve the pizza hot or cold in slices, garnished with basil sprigs.

Low-fat Calzone

Like pizza, calzone conjures up an image of sheer indulgence in terms of its fat content, but here's one you can eat with a completely clear conscience.

Makes 4

450g/1lb/4 cups plain (all-purpose) flour
pinch of salt
1 sachet easy-blend (rapid-rise) dried yeast
about 350ml/12fl oz/1 ½ cups warm water

For the filling

5ml/1 tsp olive oil, plus extra for greasing
1 medium red onion, thinly sliced
3 medium courgettes (zucchini), total weight about 350g/12oz, sliced
2 large tomatoes, diced
150g/5oz half-fat mozzarella cheese, diced
15ml/1 tbsp chopped fresh oregano, plus extra sprigs, to garnish
skimmed milk, to glaze
salt and ground black pepper

1 Sift the flour and salt into a bowl and stir in the yeast. Stir in just enough warm water to mix to a soft dough. Knead for about 5 minutes, until smooth.

2 Return the dough to the clean bowl, cover with clear film (plastic wrap) and leave in a warm place for about 1 hour, or until doubled in bulk.

3 Meanwhile, make the filling. Heat the oil. Add the onion and courgettes and cook over a low heat, stirring occasionally, for 3–4 minutes, until softened but not coloured. Remove from the heat and add the tomatoes, cheese and oregano, then season with salt and pepper to taste.

4 Preheat the oven to 220°C/425°F/Gas 7. Knead the dough lightly and divide into four pieces. Roll out each piece on a floured surface to a 20cm/8in round. Place one-quarter of the filling on one half of each round. Brush the edges of each round with milk and fold the dough over, turnover-style, to enclose the filling. Press the edges together firmly to seal. Brush each calzone with milk to glaze. Bake on a lightly oiled baking sheet for 15–20 minutes. Serve immediately.

Leek, Mushroom & Lemon Risotto

Leeks and lemon go together beautifully in this delightfully light risotto, while mushrooms add texture and extra flavour.

Serves 4

30ml/2 tbsp olive oil
3 garlic cloves, crushed
225g/8oz trimmed leeks, sliced
225g/8oz/2–3 cups brown cap
   (cremini) mushrooms, sliced

75g/3oz/6 tbsp butter
1 large onion, coarsely chopped
350g/12oz/1¾ cups risotto rice
1.2 litres/2 pints/5 cups
   simmering vegetable stock
grated rind of 1 lemon
45ml/3 tbsp lemon juice
50g/2oz/⅔ cup freshly grated
   Parmesan cheese
60ml/4 tbsp mixed chopped fresh
   chives and flat leaf parsley
salt and ground black pepper

1 Heat the olive oil in a large pan and cook the garlic for 1 minute. Add the leeks and mushrooms and season to taste with salt and pepper. Cook over a low heat, stirring occasionally, for about 10 minutes, or until the leeks have softened and browned. Spoon the mixture into a bowl and set aside.

2 Melt 25g/1oz/2 tbsp of the butter in the pan and cook the onion, stirring occasionally, for 5 minutes, until it has softened and is golden. Stir in the rice until the grains are coated, then add a ladleful of hot stock. Cook gently, stirring frequently, until all the liquid has been absorbed.

3 Continue to add the remaining stock, a little at a time, and stirring constantly. After about 25–30 minutes, the rice will have absorbed all the stock and the risotto will be moist and creamy.

4 Add the leeks and mushrooms, with the remaining butter. Stir in the lemon rind and juice, then the grated Parmesan and the herbs. Adjust the seasoning, spoon into a bowl and serve.

Cook's Tip
Always wash leeks very thoroughly, as soil and grit may be trapped within the leaves.

Nutty Rice with Mushrooms

This delicious and quite substantial supper dish can be eaten either hot, or cold with salads.

Serves 4–6

350g/12oz/1¾ cups long
   grain rice
45ml/3 tbsp sunflower oil
1 small onion, coarsely chopped
225g/8oz/3 cups field (portabello)
   mushrooms, sliced

50g/2oz/½ cup hazelnuts,
   coarsely chopped
50g/2oz/½ cup pecan nuts,
   coarsely chopped
50g/2oz/½ cup almonds,
   coarsely chopped
60ml/4 tbsp chopped
   fresh parsley
salt and ground black pepper
fresh flat leaf parsley sprigs,
   to garnish

1 Bring a large pan of water to the boil. Add the rice and cook for about 10 minutes, or until just tender. Drain, refresh under cold water and drain again. Leave to dry.

2 Heat half the oil in a wok. Add the rice and stir-fry over a medium heat for 2–3 minutes. Remove and set aside.

3 Add the remaining oil to the wok. Add the onion and stir-fry for 2 minutes, until softened, then mix in the sliced mushrooms and stir-fry for 2 minutes more.

4 Add all the nuts and stir-fry for 1 minute. Return the rice to the wok and toss over the heat for 3 minutes. Season with salt and pepper to taste. Stir in the chopped parsley and serve with a garnish of flat leaf parsley sprigs.

Cook's Tips
• *When cooking in a wok, always preheat it. When it is hot, add the oil and swirl it around to coat the sides. Then allow the oil to heat up before adding any ingredients.*
• *It is possible to stir-fry in a frying pan, if you don't have a wok. However, the heat will be less evenly distributed and it is harder to toss the ingredients without making a mess.*

Mushroom, Leek & Cashew Nut Risotto

Because this risotto is made with brown rice instead of the traditional Italian arborio rice, it has a delicious nutty flavour and interesting texture.

Serves 4
225g/8oz/1 1/3 cups long grain
   brown rice
900ml/1 1/2 pints/3 3/4 cups
   vegetable stock
15ml/1 tbsp walnut or
   hazelnut oil
2 leeks, sliced

225g/8oz/3 cups mixed
   wild and/or cultivated
   mushrooms, sliced
50g/2oz/ 1/2 cup cashew nuts
grated rind of 1 lemon
30ml/2 tbsp chopped fresh thyme
25g/1oz/scant 1/4 cup
   pumpkin seeds
salt and ground black pepper

For the garnish
fresh thyme leaves
lemon wedges

1 Place the brown rice in a large pan, pour in the stock and bring to the boil over a medium heat. Lower the heat and cook gently for about 30 minutes, until all the stock has been absorbed and the rice grains are tender.

2 About 5 minutes before the rice will be ready, heat the oil in a large, heavy frying pan. Add the leeks and mushrooms and cook over a low heat, stirring occasionally, for 3 minutes, until the leeks are softened.

3 Add the cashews, grated lemon rind and chopped thyme to the vegetable mixture and cook over a low heat, stirring frequently, for 1–2 minutes more. Season to taste with salt and pepper.

4 Drain off any excess stock from the cooked rice and stir the rice into the vegetable mixture. Turn the mixture into a warmed serving dish. Sprinkle the pumpkin seeds over the top and garnish with the fresh thyme sprigs and lemon wedges. Serve the risotto immediately.

Risotto Primavera

Celebrate springtime with this quick and easy rice dish. Use organic vegetables, if possible, so that you can really savour the flavour.

Serves 4
250g/9oz mixed spring vegetables
10ml/2 tsp olive oil
1 medium onion, sliced

250g/9oz/1 1/4 cups risotto rice
2.5ml/ 1/2 tsp ground turmeric
about 600ml/1 pint/2 1/2 cups
   vegetable stock
45ml/3 tbsp chopped
   fresh parsley
salt and ground black pepper

1 Prepare the vegetables according to type, cutting them to more or less the same size and leaving small ones whole so that they cook evenly.

2 Heat the oil in a large, non-stick pan. Add the onion and cook over a low heat, stirring occasionally, for 10 minutes, until softened and golden.

3 Stir in the rice and cook, stirring constantly, for 1–2 minutes, until the grains are all coated with oil and glistening. Add the turmeric and cook, stirring constantly, for 1 minute, then add the vegetable stock. Season well with salt and pepper. Bring to the boil, then add the vegetables.

4 Bring back to the boil, then lower the heat, cover and cook gently, stirring occasionally, for 20 minutes, or until the rice is tender and most of the liquid has been absorbed. Add more stock if necessary.

5 Stir in the parsley. Transfer the risotto to a warmed serving dish and serve immediately.

Variation
Use this risotto to stuff lightly grilled (broiled), halved red (bell) peppers, but chop the vegetables finely in step 1.

Herbed Rice Pilaff

The difference between a pilau and a pilaff is largely one of origin. Both are rice dishes, usually with spices and often including a mixture of vegetables for colour and extra flavour. This delightful dish is a simple herb mixture.

Serves 4

225g/8oz/scant 1 cup mixed brown basmati and wild rice
15ml/1 tbsp olive oil
1 onion, chopped
1 garlic clove, crushed
5ml/1 tsp ground cumin
5ml/1 tsp ground turmeric
50g/2oz/ 1/3 cup sultanas (golden raisins)
750ml/1 1/4 pints/3 cups vegetable stock
45ml/3 tbsp chopped fresh mixed herbs
salt and ground black pepper
fresh herb sprigs and 25g/1oz/ 1/4 cup chopped nuts, to garnish

1 Rinse the basmati and wild rice mixture several times in cold water until the water is clear. If there is sufficient time, leave it to soak for 30 minutes in the water used for the final rinse. Drain well.

2 Heat the oil in a large, heavy pan. Add the chopped onion and garlic and cook over a low heat, stirring occasionally, for about 5 minutes, until the onion is softened but not coloured.

3 Stir in the ground cumin, turmeric and rice and cook over a moderate heat, stirring constantly, for about 1 minute, until the rice grains are well coated.

4 Stir in the sultanas and vegetable stock. Bring to the boil, stirring frequently. Lower the heat, cover and simmer, stirring occasionally to prevent the rice from sticking to the pan, for 20–25 minutes, until the rice is cooked and just tender and almost all the liquid has been absorbed.

5 Stir in the chopped mixed herbs and season to taste with salt and pepper. Spoon the pilaff into a warmed serving dish and garnish with fresh herb sprigs and a sprinkling of chopped nuts. Serve immediately.

Fried Rice with Mushrooms

Sesame oil adds a hint of nutty flavour to this tasty and substantial rice dish.

Serves 4

225g/8oz/generous 1 cup long grain rice
15ml/1 tbsp vegetable oil
1 egg, lightly beaten
2 garlic cloves, crushed
175g/6oz/2 1/4 cups button (white) mushrooms, sliced
15ml/1 tbsp light soy sauce
1.5ml/ 1/4 tsp salt
2.5ml/ 1/2 tsp sesame oil
cucumber batons, to garnish

1 Rinse the rice until the water runs clear, then drain it thoroughly. Place it in a pan. Measure the depth of the rice against your index finger, then bring the tip of your finger up to just above the surface of the rice and add cold water to the same depth above the rice as the rice depth.

2 Bring the water to the boil. Boil, stirring constantly, for a few minutes, then cover the pan. Lower the heat to a simmer and cook the rice gently for 5–8 minutes, until all the water has been absorbed. Remove the pan from the heat and, without lifting the lid, leave for 10 minutes more.

3 Meanwhile, heat 5ml/1 tsp of the vegetable oil in a non-stick frying pan or wok. Add the beaten egg and cook, stirring with chopsticks or a wooden spoon until lightly scrambled. Remove from the pan or wok and set aside.

4 Heat the remaining vegetable oil in the pan or wok. Add the garlic and stir-fry for a few seconds, then add the mushrooms and stir-fry for 2 minutes, adding a little water, if needed, to prevent them from burning.

5 Fork through the cooked rice. Add it to the pan or wok. Toss to mix with the mushrooms, then cook for about 4 minutes, or until the rice is hot, stirring occasionally.

6 Add the scrambled egg, soy sauce, salt and sesame oil. Cook for 1 minute to heat through. Serve immediately, garnished with the cucumber batons.

Middle-Eastern Rice with Lentils

Part of the appeal of this spicy main meal dish lies in its sheer simplicity as well as the speed with which it can be cooked.

Serves 4
30ml/2 tbsp sunflower oil
1 large onion, sliced
4–5 cardamom pods
2.5ml/ 1/2 tsp coriander
   seeds, crushed
2.5ml/ 1/2 tsp cumin
   seeds, crushed

small piece of fresh root ginger,
   finely chopped
1 cinnamon stick
1 garlic clove, crushed
115g/4oz/ 3/4 cup brown rice
about 900ml/1 1/2 pints/3 3/4 cups
   vegetable stock
2.5ml/ 1/2 tsp ground turmeric
115g/4oz/ 1/2 cup split red lentils
25g/1oz/ 1/4 cup flaked (sliced)
   almonds, toasted
50g/2oz/ 1/3 cup raisins
natural (plain) yogurt, to serve

1 Heat the sunflower oil in a large, heavy pan. Add the sliced onion and cook over a medium heat, stirring occasionally, for 5 minutes, until softened.

2 Crush the cardamom pods, extract the seeds and add them to the pan, together with the coriander seeds, cumin seeds, ginger, cinnamon stick and garlic. Stir over a medium heat for 2–3 minutes.

3 Add the rice, stirring to coat the grains in the spice mixture, then pour in the stock. Stir in the turmeric. Bring to the boil, then lower the heat, cover the pan with a tight-fitting lid and simmer for 15 minutes.

4 Add the lentils to the pan, replace the lid and cook for 20 minutes more, or until the rice and lentils are tender and all the stock has been absorbed. If the mixture seems to be drying out, stir in a little more stock.

5 When all the stock has been absorbed, tip the rice mixture into a heated serving dish. Remove and discard the cinnamon stick. Sprinkle the toasted almonds and raisins over the top. Serve with the yogurt.

Quick Basmati & Nut Pilaff

Light and fragrant basmati rice cooks perfectly using this simple pilaff method.

Serves 4–6
225g/8oz/generous 1 cup
   basmati rice
15–30ml/1–2 tbsp sunflower oil
1 onion, chopped
1 garlic clove, crushed
1 large carrot, coarsely grated

5ml/1 tsp cumin seeds
10ml/2 tsp ground coriander
10ml/2 tsp black mustard seeds
4 cardamom pods
450ml/ 3/4 pint/scant 2 cups
   vegetable stock
1 bay leaf
75g/3oz/ 3/4 cup unsalted nuts
salt and ground black pepper
chopped fresh parsley or
   coriander (cilantro), to garnish

1 Rinse the rice in several changes of cold water until the water is clear. If there is sufficient time, leave it to soak for 30 minutes in the water used for the final rinse.

2 Heat the oil in a large shallow pan and cook the onion, garlic and carrot for 2–3 minutes. Stir in the rice and spices and cook for 1–2 minutes, so that the grains are coated in oil.

3 Pour in the stock, add the bay leaf and season to taste with salt and pepper. Bring to the boil, then lower the heat, cover and simmer very gently for about 10 minutes.

4 Remove from the heat without lifting the lid – this helps the rice to firm up and cook further. Leave for about 5 minutes, then check the rice. If it is cooked, there will be small steam holes in the centre. Discard the bay leaf and cardamom pods.

5 Stir in the nuts and check the seasoning. Spoon the mixture into a serving dish and sprinkle the chopped parsley or coriander over the surface. Serve immediately.

> **Cook's Tip**
> Use whatever nuts are your favourites, such as almonds, cashews or pistachios – even unsalted peanuts are good.

Vegetable Couscous with Saffron & Harissa

A North African favourite, this spicy dish makes an excellent midweek supper.

Serves 4

45ml/3 tbsp olive oil
1 onion, chopped
2 garlic cloves, crushed
5ml/1 tsp ground cumin
5ml/1 tsp paprika
400g/14oz can chopped
   tomatoes
300ml/½ pint/1¼ cups
   vegetable stock
1 cinnamon stick
generous pinch of saffron threads

4 baby aubergines
   (eggplant), quartered
8 baby courgettes (zucchini),
   trimmed and quartered
   lengthways
8 baby carrots
225g/8oz/1⅓ cups couscous
400g/14oz can chickpeas,
   drained and rinsed
175g/6oz/¾ cup prunes
45ml/3 tbsp chopped
   fresh parsley
45ml/3 tbsp chopped fresh
   coriander (cilantro)
10–15ml/2–3 tsp harissa
salt

1 Heat the oil in a large pan and cook the onion and garlic for 5 minutes, until soft. Add the cumin and paprika and cook, stirring, for 1 minute. Stir in the tomatoes, stock, cinnamon stick, saffron, aubergines, courgettes and carrots. Season with salt. Bring to the boil, cover and cook gently for 20 minutes.

2 Select a colander that will fit over the pan of vegetables. Line it with a double thickness of muslin (cheesecloth). Soak the couscous according to the instructions on the packet.

3 Add the chickpeas and prunes to the vegetables and cook for 5 minutes. Fork the couscous to break up any lumps and spread it in the colander. Place it on top of the vegetables, cover, and cook for 5 minutes until the couscous is hot.

4 Tip the couscous into a warmed dish. Using a slotted spoon, add the vegetables. Spoon over a little of the cooking liquid, add the parsley and coriander and toss gently to combine. Stir the harissa into the remaining sauce and serve separately.

Spiced Couscous with Halloumi

Courgette ribbons add colour and flavour to this delicious dish.

Serves 4

275g/10oz/1⅔ cups couscous
500ml/17fl oz/generous 2 cups
   boiling water
1 bay leaf
1 cinnamon stick
30ml/2 tbsp olive oil, plus extra
   for brushing
1 large red onion, chopped
2 garlic cloves, chopped

5ml/1 tsp mild chilli powder
5ml/1 tsp ground cumin
5ml/1 tsp ground coriander
5 cardamom pods, bruised
50g/2oz/⅓ cup whole blanched
   almonds, toasted
1 peach, stoned (pitted) and diced
25g/1oz/2 tbsp butter
3 courgettes (zucchini), sliced
   lengthways into ribbons
225g/8oz Halloumi cheese, sliced
salt and ground black pepper
chopped fresh flat leaf parsley,
   to garnish

1 Place the couscous in a bowl and pour over the boiling water. Add the bay leaf and cinnamon stick and season with salt. Leave the couscous for 10 minutes.

2 Meanwhile, heat the oil in a large, heavy pan and cook the onion and garlic until the onion has softened, stirring occasionally. Stir in the chilli powder, cumin, coriander and cardamom pods and cook for a further 3 minutes.

3 Fork the couscous to break up any lumps, then add it to the pan, with the almonds, diced peach and butter. Heat through for 2 minutes.

4 Brush a griddle pan with olive oil and heat until very hot. Turn down the heat to medium, then place the courgettes on the griddle and cook for 5 minutes, until tender and slightly charred. Turn them over, add the Halloumi and continue cooking for 5 minutes more, turning the Halloumi halfway through.

5 Remove the cinnamon stick, bay leaf and cardamom pods from the couscous mixture, then pile it on a plate and season to taste with salt and pepper. Top with the Halloumi and courgettes. Sprinkle the parsley over the top and serve.

Aubergine & Chickpea Tagine

Spiced with coriander, cumin, cinnamon, turmeric and a dash of chilli sauce, this Moroccan-style stew makes a filling supper dish.

Serves 4

1 small aubergine (eggplant), cut into 1cm/½in dice
2 courgettes (zucchini), thickly sliced
30ml/2 tbsp olive oil
1 large onion, sliced
2 garlic cloves, chopped
150g/5oz/2 cups brown cap (cremini) mushrooms, halved
15ml/1 tbsp ground coriander
10ml/2 tsp cumin seeds
15ml/1 tbsp ground cinnamon
10ml/2 tsp ground turmeric
225g/8oz new potatoes, quartered
600ml/1 pint/2½ cups passata (bottled strained tomatoes)
15ml/1 tbsp tomato purée (paste)
150ml/¼ pint/⅔ cup water
15ml/1 tbsp chilli sauce
8 ready-to-eat dried apricots
400g/14oz can chickpeas, drained and rinsed
salt and ground black pepper
15ml/1 tbsp chopped fresh coriander (cilantro), to garnish
rice, to serve

1 Put the aubergine and courgettes in a colander, sprinkling salt over each layer. Leave to stand in the sink for 30 minutes. Rinse very well, drain and pat dry with kitchen paper.

2 Preheat the grill (broiler). Arrange the courgettes and aubergine on a baking sheet and toss in half the olive oil. Grill (broil) for 20 minutes, turning occasionally, until golden.

3 Heat the remaining oil in a large pan and cook the onion and garlic until softened. Add the mushrooms and cook for 3 minutes. Add the spices and stir over the heat for 1 minute. Add the potatoes and cook for 3 minutes, stirring. Pour in the passata, tomato purée and water and cook for 10 minutes, or until the sauce begins to thicken.

4 Add the aubergine, courgettes, chilli sauce, apricots and chickpeas. Season to taste and cook, partially covered, for 10–15 minutes, until the potatoes are tender. Sprinkle with chopped fresh coriander and serve with rice.

Purée of Lentils with Baked Eggs

This unusual dish makes an excellent vegetarian supper. If you like, and have one big enough, bake the purée and eggs in a single large ovenproof dish.

Serves 4

450g/1lb/2 cups split red lentils
3 leeks, thinly sliced
10ml/2 tsp coriander seeds, finely crushed
15ml/1 tbsp chopped fresh coriander (cilantro)
30ml/2 tbsp chopped fresh mint
15ml/1 tbsp red wine vinegar
1 litre/1¾ pints/4 cups vegetable stock
vegetable oil, for greasing
4 eggs
salt and ground black pepper
generous handful of fresh parsley, chopped, to garnish

1 Put the lentils in a deep pan. Add the leeks, coriander seeds, fresh coriander, mint, vinegar and stock. Bring to the boil over a medium heat. Lower the heat, cover and simmer for about 30–40 minutes, or until the lentils are cooked and have absorbed all the liquid.

2 Preheat the oven to 180°C/350°F/Gas 4. Lightly grease four individual ovenproof dishes. Season the lentil mixture to taste with salt and pepper and mix thoroughly. Divide the mixture among the prepared dishes and spread out.

3 Using the back of a tablespoon, make a fairly small depression in the centre of the lentil mixture in each dish. Break an egg into each hollow. Season the eggs lightly with salt and pepper. Cover the dishes with foil and bake for 15–20 minutes, or until the eggs are set. Sprinkle with plenty of chopped parsley and serve immediately.

Variation
Tip a 400g/14oz can of unsweetened chestnut purée into a bowl and beat well until softened. Stir the purée into the lentil mixture in step 2, with a little extra vegetable stock if required. Proceed as in the main recipe.

Braised Barley & Vegetables

One of the oldest cultivated cereals, pot barley has a nutty colour and slightly chewy texture. It makes a warming and filling dish when combined with a selection of root vegetables.

Serves 4

30ml/2 tbsp sunflower oil
1 large onion, chopped
2 celery sticks, sliced
2 carrots, halved lengthways
   and sliced
225g/8oz/1 cup pearl or
   pot barley
1 large piece of swede (rutabaga),
   about 225g/8oz, cubed
1 large potato, about 225g/
   8oz, cubed
475ml/16fl oz/2 cups
   vegetable stock
salt and ground black pepper
celery leaves, to garnish

1 Heat the oil in a large pan. Add the onion and cook over a low heat, stirring occasionally, for 5 minutes, until softened. Add the sliced celery and carrots and cook for 3–4 minutes, or until the onion is starting to brown.

2 Add the barley, then stir in the swede and potato. Pour in the stock and season to taste with salt and pepper. Bring to the boil, then lower the heat and cover the pan.

3 Simmer, stirring occasionally, for 40 minutes, or until most of the stock has been absorbed and the barley is tender.

4 Spoon on to warmed serving plates, garnish with the celery leaves and serve.

Variations
• *This tastes good with feta cheese, especially if you use the cubes that are conveniently packed in oil. Toss them into the mixture just before serving and drizzle over a little of the oil from the jar, if you like.*
• *You can substitute or add other vegetables, such as celeriac or parsnips. For a more summery version of the dish, use fennel, courgettes (zucchini) and broad (fava) beans.*

Beetroot Casserole

Maybe beetroot isn't the obvious choice for a casserole, but this sweet and sour dish is delicious.

Serves 4

50g/2oz/¼ cup butter
1 onion, chopped
2 garlic cloves, crushed
675g/1½ lb raw beetroot (beet),
   peeled and diced
2 large carrots, diced
115g/4oz/1½ cups button
   (white) mushrooms
300ml/½ pint/1¼ cups
   vegetable stock
grated rind and juice of ½ lemon
2 bay leaves
15ml/1 tbsp chopped fresh mint
salt and ground black pepper

For the hot dressing
150ml/¼ pint/²⁄₃ cup
   sour cream
2.5ml/½ tsp paprika, plus extra
   to garnish

1 Melt the butter in a non-aluminium pan. Add the onion and garlic and cook over a low heat for 5 minutes. Add the beetroot, carrots and mushrooms and cook for 5 minutes more. Pour in the stock, then add the lemon rind and bay leaves. Season with salt and pepper. Bring to the boil, lower the heat, cover and simmer for 1 hour, until the vegetables are soft.

2 Turn off the heat and stir in the lemon juice and mint. Cover the pan and leave it to stand for 5 minutes.

3 Meanwhile, make the dressing. Gently heat the sour cream and paprika in a small pan, stirring constantly, until bubbling.

4 Transfer the beetroot mixture to a serving bowl, spoon over the dressing and sprinkle with a little more paprika. Serve.

Cook's Tips
• *Wear rubber or plastic gloves to avoid staining your hands when preparing beetroot (beet).*
• *Cooking beetroot in an aluminium pan may cause discoloration of the pan and food.*

Harvest Vegetable & Lentil Casserole

In autumn, thoughts turn to hearty, satisfying food. This sustaining, yet low-fat dish is the ideal choice.

Serves 6
15ml/1 tbsp sunflower oil
2 leeks, sliced
1 garlic clove, crushed
4 celery sticks, chopped
2 carrots, sliced
2 parsnips, diced
1 sweet potato, diced
225g/8oz swede (rutabaga), diced

175g/6oz/ ¾ cup whole brown or
   green lentils
450g/1lb tomatoes, peeled,
   seeded and chopped
15ml/1 tbsp chopped fresh thyme
15ml/1 tbsp chopped
   fresh marjoram
900ml/1½ pints/3¾ cups
   vegetable stock
15ml/1 tbsp cornflour
   (cornstarch)
45ml/3 tbsp water
salt and ground black pepper
fresh thyme sprigs, to garnish

1 Preheat the oven to 180°C/350°F/Gas 4. Heat the oil in a large flameproof casserole. Add the leeks, garlic and celery and cook over a low heat, stirring occasionally, for 3 minutes, until the onion is beginning to soften.

2 Add the carrots, parsnips, sweet potato, swede, lentils, tomatoes, herbs and stock. Stir well and season with salt and pepper to taste. Bring to the boil, stirring occasionally.

3 Cover the casserole, transfer it to the oven and bake for about 50 minutes, until the vegetables and lentils are tender, stirring the vegetable mixture once or twice.

4 Remove the casserole from the oven. Blend the cornflour with the water in a small bowl. Stir the mixture into the casserole and heat it gently on the hob (stovetop), stirring constantly, until the mixture boils and thickens. Lower the heat and simmer gently for 2 minutes, stirring.

5 Spoon on to warmed serving plates or into bowls, garnish with the thyme sprigs and serve.

Mushroom & Fennel Hot-pot

Marvellous flavours permeate this unusual main course, which makes the most of both dried and fresh mushrooms.

Serves 4
25g/1oz/2 cups dried
   shiitake mushrooms
30ml/2 tbsp olive oil
12 shallots, peeled and left whole
1 small head of fennel,
   coarsely chopped

225g/8oz/3 cups button (white)
   mushrooms, halved
300ml/ ½ pint/1¼ cups dry
   (hard) cider
2 large pieces sun-dried tomatoes
   in oil, drained and sliced
30ml/2 tbsp sun-dried
   tomato paste
1 bay leaf
chopped fresh parsley,
   to garnish

1 Place the dried mushrooms in a bowl. Pour over boiling water to cover and set aside for 20 minutes. Drain, reserving the liquid. Discard the stalks and chop the caps into pieces.

2 Heat the oil in a flameproof casserole. Add the shallots and fennel and cook over a low heat, stirring occasionally, for 10 minutes, or until the vegetables have softened.

3 Add the button mushrooms and cook for 2–3 minutes, then stir in the shiitake mushrooms and cook for 1 minute more. Pour in the cider and stir in the sun-dried tomatoes and sun-dried tomato paste. Add the bay leaf. Bring to the boil, then lower the heat, cover the casserole and simmer gently for about 30 minutes.

4 If the mixture seems dry, stir in the reserved liquid from the soaked mushrooms. Reheat briefly, then remove the bay leaf and serve, sprinkled with plenty of chopped parsley.

Cook's Tip
Dried mushrooms swell up a great deal after soaking, so a little goes a long way in terms of both flavour and quantity.

Bean Feast with Mexican Salsa

Canned beans really come into their own when you need to make a nutritious meal in double-quick time.

Serves 4

400g/14oz can red kidney beans
400g/14oz can flageolet or small
   cannellini beans
400g/14oz can borlotti beans
15ml/1 tbsp olive oil
1 small onion, finely chopped
3 garlic cloves, finely chopped
1 fresh red chilli, seeded and
   finely chopped
1 red (bell) pepper, seeded and
   coarsely chopped
2 bay leaves
10ml/2 tsp chopped
   fresh oregano
10ml/2 tsp ground cumin
5ml/1 tsp ground coriander
2.5ml/½ tsp ground cloves
15ml/1 tbsp soft dark
   brown sugar
300ml/½ pint/1¼ cups
   vegetable stock
salt and ground black pepper
fresh coriander (cilantro) sprigs,
   to garnish

For the salsa

1 ripe but firm avocado
45ml/3 tbsp freshly squeezed
   lime juice
1 small red onion, chopped
1 small fresh hot green chilli,
   thinly sliced
3 ripe plum tomatoes, peeled,
   seeded and chopped
45ml/3 tbsp chopped fresh
   coriander (cilantro)

1 Drain all the beans in a colander and rinse thoroughly. Heat the oil in a heavy pan. Add the onion and cook over a low heat, stirring occasionally, for 3 minutes, until soft and transparent. Add the garlic, chilli, red pepper, bay leaves, oregano, cumin, coriander and cloves. Stir well and cook for a further 3 minutes, then add the sugar, beans and stock and cook for 8 minutes. Season with salt and pepper and leave over a low heat while you make the salsa.

2 Cut the avocado in half, remove the stone (pit), then peel it and dice the flesh. Toss it with the lime juice, then add all the remaining salsa ingredients and season with plenty of black pepper. Mix well.

3 Spoon the beans into four serving bowls. Garnish with sprigs of fresh coriander and serve with the salsa.

Tuscan Baked Beans

Cannellini beans are delicious with garlic and sage in this tasty baked dish, which can be served hot or at room temperature.

Serves 6–8

600g/1lb 6oz/3½ cups dried
   cannellini beans
60ml/4 tbsp olive oil
2 garlic cloves, crushed
3 fresh sage leaves
1 leek, thinly sliced
400g/14oz can
   chopped tomatoes
salt and ground black pepper

1 Carefully pick over the beans, place them in a large bowl and cover with water. Soak for at least 6 hours, or overnight.

2 Preheat the oven to 180°C/350°F/Gas 4. Heat the oil in a small pan. Add the garlic cloves and sage leaves and cook over a low heat, stirring occasionally, for 3–4 minutes. Remove the pan from the heat.

3 Drain the cannellini beans and put them in a pan with cold water to cover. Bring to the boil and boil vigorously for 10 minutes. Drain again.

4 Tip the beans into a casserole and add the leek and tomatoes. Stir in the garlic and sage, with the oil in which they were cooked. Add enough cold water to cover the beans by 2.5cm/1in. Mix well. Cover the casserole and bake for 1¾ hours.

5 Remove the casserole from the oven, stir the bean mixture, and season to taste with salt and pepper. Return the casserole to the oven, uncovered, and cook for 15 minutes more, until the beans are tender. Remove from the oven and leave to stand for 7–8 minutes before serving.

Cook's Tip
Cannellini beans are also known as Italian haricot beans.

Jamaican Black Bean Pot

Molasses imparts a rich treacly flavour to the spicy sauce, which includes black beans, vibrant red and yellow peppers and melting butternut squash.

Serves 4
225g/8oz/1¼ cups dried black
    beans, soaked overnight in
    water to cover
1 bay leaf
5ml/1 tsp vegetable stock
    (bouillon) powder
15ml/1 tbsp sunflower oil
1 large onion, chopped
1 garlic clove, chopped

5ml/1 tsp English (hot)
    mustard powder
15ml/1 tbsp blackstrap molasses
30ml/2 tbsp soft dark
    brown sugar
5ml/1 tsp dried thyme
2.5ml/½ tsp dried chilli flakes
1 red (bell) pepper, seeded
    and diced
1 yellow (bell) pepper, seeded
    and diced
675g/1½lb butternut squash,
    seeded and cut into 1cm/
    ½in dice
salt and ground black pepper
fresh thyme sprigs, to garnish
cooked rice, to serve

1 Drain the beans, rinse them well and drain them again. Place them in a large pan, cover with fresh water and add the bay leaf. Bring to the boil, then boil rapidly for 10 minutes. Lower the heat, cover, and simmer for 30 minutes, until tender.

2 Drain the beans, reserving the cooking liquid in a large measuring jug (cup). Stir in the stock powder, then make the liquid up to 400ml/14fl oz/1⅔ cups with water. Preheat the oven to 180°C/350°F/Gas 4.

3 Heat the oil in the pan. Add the onion and garlic and cook over a low heat, stirring occasionally, for about 5 minutes, until softened. Stir in the mustard powder, molasses, sugar, dried thyme and chilli flakes. Cook for 1 minute, stirring.

4 Stir in the black beans and reserved stock. Spoon the mixture into a casserole. Cover and bake for 25 minutes, then add the peppers and squash. Season to taste and mix well. Replace the lid and bake for 45 minutes more, until the vegetables are tender. Serve, garnished with thyme sprigs, accompanied by rice.

Sweet & Sour Bean Hot-pot

An appetizing mixture of mixed beans and vegetables in a tasty sweet and sour sauce, topped with a golden potato crust.

Serves 6
450g/1lb potatoes
15ml/1 tbsp olive oil
40g/1½oz/3 tbsp half-fat spread
40g/1½oz/6 tbsp wholemeal
    (whole-wheat) flour
300ml/½ pint/1¼ cups passata
    (bottled strained tomatoes)
150ml/¼ pint/⅔ cup
    unsweetened apple juice
60ml/4 tbsp light brown sugar
60ml/4 tbsp tomato ketchup
60ml/4 tbsp dry sherry

60 ml/4 tbsp cider vinegar
60ml/4 tbsp light soy sauce
400g/14oz can butter
    (lima) beans
400g/14oz can red kidney beans
400g/14oz can flageolet or small
    cannellini beans
400g/14oz can chickpeas
175g/6oz green beans, chopped
    and blanched
225g/8oz shallots, sliced
    and blanched
225g/8oz/3 cups
    mushrooms, sliced
15ml/1 tbsp chopped fresh thyme
15ml/1 tbsp chopped
    fresh marjoram
salt and ground black pepper
fresh herb sprigs, to garnish

1 Preheat the oven to 200°C/400°F/Gas 6. Bring a pan of water to the boil and par-boil the potatoes for 4 minutes. Drain well, toss in the oil to coat all over and set them aside.

2 Mix the half-fat spread, flour, passata, apple juice, sugar, tomato ketchup, sherry, vinegar and soy sauce in a pan. Heat gently, whisking constantly, until the sauce comes to the boil and thickens. Simmer gently for 3 minutes, stirring.

3 Rinse and drain the canned pulses and add to the sauce with the remaining ingredients, except the herb garnish. Mix, then tip into an ovenproof dish and level the surface.

4 Arrange the potato slices over the top, overlapping them slightly and covering the bean mixture completely. Cover with foil and bake for 40 minutes. Remove the foil and bake for 20 minutes more, until the potatoes have begun to brown around the edges. Serve, garnished with fresh herbs.

Spicy Chickpeas with Fresh Ginger

Here's another excellent chickpea recipe, this time with ginger, spring onions and fresh mint.

Serves 4–6
30ml/2 tbsp vegetable oil
1 small onion, chopped
4cm/1½in piece of fresh root ginger, finely chopped
2 garlic cloves, finely chopped
1.5ml/¼ tsp ground turmeric
450g/1lb tomatoes, peeled, seeded and chopped
2 x 400g/14oz cans chickpeas, drained
30ml/2 tbsp chopped fresh coriander (cilantro)
10ml/2 tsp garam masala
salt and ground black pepper
fresh coriander (cilantro) sprigs, to garnish

For the raita
150ml/¼ pint/⅔ cup natural (plain) yogurt
2 spring onions (scallions), finely chopped
5ml/1 tsp roasted cumin seeds
30ml/2 tbsp chopped fresh mint
pinch of cayenne pepper

1 Heat the oil in a large pan. Add the onion and cook over a low heat, stirring occasionally, for 2–3 minutes. Add the ginger, garlic and turmeric. Cook for a few seconds more.

2 Stir in the tomatoes and chickpeas and season with salt and pepper to taste. Bring to the boil, then simmer for 10–15 minutes, until the mixture has reduced to a thick sauce.

3 Meanwhile, make the raita. Mix the yogurt, spring onions, roasted cumin seeds, mint and cayenne pepper in a small serving bowl. Set aside.

4 Just before the end of cooking, stir the chopped coriander and garam masala into the chickpea mixture. Serve immediately, garnished with coriander sprigs and accompanied by the raita.

> **Variation**
> Try this with drained canned beans, if you like. Butter (lima) beans make an interesting alternative to chickpeas.

Curried Spinach & Chickpeas

Serve this with yogurt and naan bread, for a satisfying and very tasty meal.

Serves 6
30ml/2 tbsp vegetable oil
2 garlic cloves, crushed
1 onion, coarsely chopped
30ml/2 tbsp medium curry paste
15ml/1 tbsp black mustard seeds
450g/1lb potatoes, diced
475ml/16fl oz/2 cups water
450g/1lb frozen leaf spinach, thawed
400g/14oz can chickpeas, drained
225g/8oz Halloumi cheese, cubed
15ml/1 tbsp freshly squeezed lime juice
salt and ground black pepper
fresh coriander (cilantro) sprigs, to garnish

1 Heat the oil in a large, heavy pan. Add the garlic and onion and cook over a medium heat, stirring occasionally, for about 5 minutes, until softened. Stir in the curry paste and mustard seeds and cook the mixture for 1 minute.

2 Add the diced potatoes and pour in the measured water. Bring to the boil and cook gently, stirring occasionally, for 20–25 minutes, until the potatoes are almost tender and most of the liquid has evaporated.

3 Meanwhile, place the thawed spinach in a sieve and press out as much liquid as possible. Chop it coarsely, then stir it into the potato mixture, with the chickpeas. Cook for 5 minutes, or until the potatoes are tender, stirring frequently.

4 Stir in the cheese cubes and lime juice, season to taste with salt and pepper and serve immediately, garnished with sprigs of fresh coriander.

> **Cook's Tip**
> In India, paneer, rather than Halloumi, would be used. This cheese is made at home by curdling boiled milk with vinegar or lemon juice, straining the curds and then pressing them with a weight for a short while.

Chilli Cheese Tortilla with Salsa

Good warm or cold, this is like a quiche without the pastry base. Cheese and chillies are more than a match for each other.

Serves 4
45ml/3 tbsp olive oil
I small onion, thinly sliced
2–3 fresh green jalapeño chillies, sliced
200g/7oz cold cooked potato, thinly sliced
130g/4¼ oz/generous I cup grated Cheddar cheese

6 eggs, beaten
salt and ground black pepper
fresh herbs, to garnish

For the salsa
500g/1¼lb tomatoes, peeled, seeded and finely chopped
I fresh mild green chilli, seeded and finely chopped
2 garlic cloves, crushed
45ml/3 tbsp chopped fresh coriander (cilantro)
juice of I lime
2.5ml/ ½ tsp salt

I First, make the salsa. Put the tomatoes in a bowl and add the chilli, garlic, coriander, lime juice and salt. Mix well and set aside.

2 Heat half the oil in a large omelette pan and gently cook the onion and jalapeños, stirring occasionally, for 5 minutes, until softened. Add the potato and cook for 5 minutes more, until lightly browned, taking care to keep the slices whole.

3 Using a slotted spoon, transfer the vegetables to a warm plate. Wipe the pan with kitchen paper, then pour in the remaining oil. Heat well, return the vegetable mixture to the pan and season to taste. Sprinkle the cheese over the top.

4 Pour in the eggs, making sure that they seep under the vegetables. Cook over a low heat until set. Serve in wedges, garnished with fresh herbs, with the salsa on the side.

Cook's Tip
If you use a frying pan with a flameproof handle, you can brown the top of the tortilla under a hot grill (broiler).

Rice & Beans with Avocado Salsa

Mexican-style rice and beans make a tasty supper dish.

Serves 4
4 tomatoes, halved and seeded
2 garlic cloves, chopped
I onion, sliced
45ml/3 tbsp olive oil
225g/8oz/generous I cup long grain brown rice, rinsed
600ml/1 pint/2½ cups vegetable stock
75g/3oz/ ½ cup canned kidney beans, rinsed and drained

2 carrots, diced
75g/3oz green beans
salt and ground black pepper
4 wheat tortillas and sour cream, to serve
15ml/1 tbsp chopped fresh coriander (cilantro), to garnish

For the salsa
I avocado
juice of I lime
I small red onion, diced
I small fresh red chilli, seeded and chopped

I Preheat the grill (broiler). Spread out the tomatoes, garlic and onion in a grill pan. Pour over 15ml/1 tbsp of the oil and toss to coat. Grill (broil) for 10 minutes, turning once. Set aside to cool.

2 Heat the remaining oil in a pan, add the rice and cook for about 2 minutes, stirring constantly, until light golden.

3 Process the cooked tomato mixture in a food processor or blender, then scrape into the rice and cook for 2 minutes more, stirring frequently. Pour in the stock, cover and cook gently for 20 minutes, stirring occasionally.

4 Reserve 30ml/2 tbsp of the kidney beans for the salsa. Add the rest to the rice mixture with the carrots and green beans. Cook for 10 minutes, until the vegetables are tender. Season well. Remove the pan from the heat and leave to stand, covered, for 15 minutes.

5 Make the salsa. Halve and stone (pit) the avocado. Peel and dice the flesh, then toss it in the lime juice. Add the onion, chilli and reserved kidney beans, then season with salt. To serve, spoon the hot rice and beans on to warm tortillas and sprinkle with the coriander. Hand around the salsa and sour cream.

Spring Vegetable Omelette

This resembles a Spanish omelette in that it is not flipped, but finished off under the grill. Packed with tender vegetables, it makes a very tasty light lunch.

Serves 4
50g/2oz/ ½ cup fresh
   asparagus tips
50g/2oz spring greens
   (collards), shredded
15ml/1 tbsp sunflower oil
1 onion, sliced
175g/6oz cooked new potatoes,
   halved or diced
2 tomatoes, chopped
6 eggs
15–30ml/1–2 tbsp chopped fresh
   mixed herbs
salt and ground black pepper
salad, to serve

1 Steam the asparagus tips and spring greens over a pan of boiling water for 5–10 minutes, until tender. Drain the vegetables and keep them warm.

2 Heat the oil in a large frying pan that can safely be used under the grill (broiler). (Cover a wooden handle with foil to protect it.) Add the onion and cook over a low heat, stirring occasionally, for 5–10 minutes, until softened.

3 Add the new potatoes and cook, stirring constantly for approximately 3 minutes. Stir in the tomatoes, asparagus and spring greens. Beat the eggs lightly with the herbs and season to taste with salt and pepper.

4 Preheat the grill. Pour the egg mixture over the vegetables, then cook over a low heat until the base of the omelette is golden brown. Slide the pan under the grill and cook the omelette for 2–3 minutes, until the top is golden brown. Serve immediately, cut into wedges, with salad.

Variation
This dish is equally delicious made with other vegetables, such as broccoli, mushrooms or leeks.

Mushroom & Sunflower Seed Flan

Mushrooms, baby corn and spinach make a delectable filling for a flan.

Serves 6
175g/6oz/1 ½ cups wholemeal
   (whole-wheat) flour
75g/3oz/6 tbsp low-fat spread
15ml/1 tbsp olive oil
175g/6oz baby corn cobs, each
   cut into 2–3 pieces
30ml/2 tbsp sunflower seeds
225g/8oz/3 cups mushrooms
75g/3oz fresh spinach
   leaves, chopped
juice of 1 lemon
salt and ground black pepper
tomato salad, to serve

1 Preheat the oven to 180°C/350°F/Gas 4. Sift the flour into a bowl, then tip in the bran from the sieve. Rub in the low-fat spread until the mixture resembles breadcrumbs. Add enough water to make a firm dough.

2 Roll out the dough on a lightly floured surface and line a 23cm/9in flan dish (quiche pan). Prick the base, line the flan case (pie shell) with foil and add a layer of baking beans. Bake blind for 15 minutes, then remove the foil and beans. Return the pastry case to the oven and bake for 10 minutes more, or until the pastry is crisp and golden brown.

3 Meanwhile, heat the oil in a heavy pan. Add the corn with the sunflower seeds and cook, stirring occasionally, for 5–8 minutes, until lightly browned all over.

4 Add the mushrooms, lower the heat slightly and cook the mixture for 2–3 minutes. Stir in the chopped spinach, cover the pan and cook for 2–3 minutes.

5 Sharpen the filling with a little lemon juice. Stir in salt and pepper to taste. Spoon into the flan case. Serve warm or cold, with a tomato salad.

Cook's Tip
If the mushrooms are large, cut them in half or quarters.

SPECIAL OCCASION DISHES

Planning a special occasion meal can be tricky. Naturally, you want the food to be impressive and memorable, but you don't want to be slaving over the hot stove all evening while everyone else is having fun. There are several ways of avoiding this and this collection of recipes provides you with all the options. You can choose a dish, such as Californian Citrus Fried Rice, that is quick to prepare and cook. An alternative is to serve a dish, such as Roasted Gem Squash, which can be prepared in advance and popped in the oven just before your guests arrive. You are then free to serve drinks and chat, while everyone savours the appetizing aroma emerging from the kitchen.

A third way is a combination of the first two. Choose a main course, such as Red Pepper & Watercress Filo Purses, where part of the preparation can be done in advance, a little attention is required after your guests arrive and then you can rejoin them while the assembled dish is cooking. Perhaps the easiest option of all is to prepare and cook the whole dish in advance and either serve it cold or, as with Cheese, Onion & Mushroom Flan, fashionably warm. This is the ideal choice when you are entertaining single-handedly and need to be chef, waiter and sparkling host simultaneously.

While all the recipes here are great for entertaining, they are still packed with goodness, high in fibre and low in saturated fats. Inviting guests doesn't mean that you have to abandon your healthy eating plan – the dishes are so delicious that everyone will enjoy them. You don't even have to worry if you are watching your weight, as there are plenty of low-fat options, such as Vegetable Paella and Ratatouille Pancakes.

Vegetable Stew with Roasted Tomato & Garlic Sauce

This lightly-spiced, richly flavoured stew makes a perfect match for couscous.

Serves 6
45ml/3 tbsp olive oil
250g/9oz shallots
1 large onion, chopped
2 garlic cloves, chopped
5ml/1 tsp cumin seeds
5ml/1 tsp ground coriander seeds
5ml/1 tsp paprika
10cm/4in piece of cinnamon stick
2 fresh bay leaves
about 450ml/³⁄₄ pint/scant 2 cups vegetable stock
good pinch of saffron threads
450g/1lb carrots, thickly sliced
2 green (bell) peppers, seeded and thickly sliced
115g/4oz/¹⁄₂ cup ready-to-eat dried apricots, halved if large
5–7.5ml/1–1¹⁄₂ tsp ground toasted cumin seeds
450g/1lb squash, peeled, seeded and cut into chunks
salt and ground black pepper
45ml/3 tbsp fresh coriander (cilantro) leaves, to garnish

For the sauce
1kg/2¹⁄₄lb tomatoes, halved
about 5ml/1 tsp granulated sugar
45ml/3 tbsp olive oil
1–2 fresh red chillies, seeded and chopped
2–3 garlic cloves, chopped
5ml/1 tsp fresh thyme leaves

1 Preheat the oven to 180°C/350°F/Gas 4. First make the sauce. Place the tomatoes, cut sides uppermost, in an ovenproof dish. Season with salt and pepper to taste, sprinkle the sugar over the top, then drizzle with the olive oil. Roast for 30 minutes.

2 Sprinkle the chillies, garlic and thyme over the tomatoes. Stir, then roast for a further 30–45 minutes, until the tomatoes have collapsed, but are still a little juicy. Cool, then process in a food processor or blender to make a thick sauce. Sieve to remove the seeds.

3 Heat 30ml/2 tbsp of the oil in a large, deep, frying pan. Add the shallots and cook over a low heat, stirring frequently, until browned all over. Remove them from the pan and set aside.

4 Add the chopped onion to the pan and cook over a low heat, stirring occasionally, for 5–7 minutes, until softened. Stir in the garlic and cumin seeds and cook for 3–4 minutes more.

5 Add the ground coriander seeds, paprika, cinnamon stick and bay leaves. Cook, stirring constantly, for 2 minutes, then mix in the stock, saffron, carrots and green peppers. Season well with salt and pepper, cover and simmer gently for 10 minutes.

6 Stir in the apricots, 5ml/1 tsp of the ground toasted cumin, the browned shallots and the squash. Stir in the tomato sauce. Cover and cook for a further 5 minutes.

7 Uncover the pan and continue to cook, stirring occasionally, for 10–15 minutes, until the vegetables are all fully cooked. Adjust the seasoning, adding more cumin and a pinch of sugar to taste. Remove and discard the cinnamon stick and bay leaves. Serve, sprinkled with the fresh coriander leaves.

Roasted Vegetables with Salsa Verde

Fresh herbs are at the heart of the Italian salsa verde – green sauce. It tastes wonderful with the vegetable mixture. Serve it with rice or a mixture of rice and vermicelli.

Serves 4
3 courgettes (zucchini), sliced lengthways
1 large fennel bulb, cut into wedges
450g/1lb butternut squash, cut into 2cm/³⁄₄in chunks
12 shallots
2 red (bell) peppers, seeded and thickly sliced
4 plum tomatoes, halved and seeded
45ml/3 tbsp olive oil
2 garlic cloves, crushed
5ml/1 tsp balsamic vinegar
salt and ground black pepper

For the salsa verde
45ml/3 tbsp chopped fresh mint
90ml/6 tbsp chopped fresh flat leaf parsley
15ml/1 tbsp Dijon mustard
juice of ¹⁄₂ lemon
30ml/2 tbsp olive oil

1 Preheat the oven to 220°C/425°F/Gas 7. Make the salsa verde. Place all the ingredients, except the olive oil, in a food processor or blender. Process to a coarse paste, then add the oil, a little at a time, until the mixture forms a smooth purée. Season to taste with salt and pepper.

2 In a large bowl, toss the courgettes, fennel, squash, shallots, red peppers and tomatoes in the olive oil, garlic and balsamic vinegar. Leave for 10 minutes to allow the flavours to mingle.

3 Place all the vegetables – apart from the squash and tomatoes – in a roasting pan. Brush with half the oil and vinegar mixture and season with plenty of salt and pepper.

4 Roast for 25 minutes. Remove the roasting pan from the oven, turn the vegetables over and brush with the rest of the oil and vinegar mixture. Add the squash and tomatoes and cook for 20–25 minutes more, until all the vegetables are tender and lightly charred around the edges. Spoon the roasted vegetables on to a warmed serving platter and serve immediately with the salsa verde.

Carrot Mousse with Mushroom Sauce

This impressive yet easy-to-make mousse makes healthy eating a pleasure.

Serves 4
about 350g/12oz carrots, coarsely chopped
1 small red (bell) pepper, seeded and coarsely chopped
45ml/3 tbsp vegetable stock
2 eggs, plus 1 egg white
115g/4oz/ ½ cup low-fat soft cheese

15ml/1 tbsp chopped fresh tarragon
salt and ground black pepper
fresh tarragon sprigs, to garnish
boiled rice and leeks, to serve

For the mushroom sauce
25g/1oz/2 tbsp low-fat spread
175g/6oz/2¼ cups mushrooms, sliced
30ml/2 tbsp plain (all-purpose) flour
250ml/8fl oz/1 cup skimmed milk

1 Preheat the oven to 190°C/375°F/Gas 5. Line the bases of four dariole moulds or ramekins with baking parchment. Put the carrots, red pepper and stock in a small pan and bring to the boil. Cover and cook for 5 minutes, or until tender. Drain.

2 Lightly beat the eggs and egg white. Mix with the soft cheese and season to taste. Process the cooked vegetables in a food processor or blender. Add the cheese mixture and process for a few seconds more, until smooth. Stir in the chopped tarragon.

3 Divide the mixture among the moulds or ramekins and cover with foil. Place in a roasting pan and pour in boiling water to come halfway up the sides. Bake for 35 minutes, or until set.

4 Make the sauce. Melt 15g/ ½oz/1 tbsp of the low-fat spread in a frying pan. Cook the mushrooms for 5 minutes, until soft. Put the remaining low-fat spread in a small pan and add the flour and milk. Cook over a medium heat, stirring until the sauce thickens. Stir in the mushrooms and season to taste.

5 Turn out each mousse on to a plate. Spoon over a little sauce and garnish with the tarragon. Serve with rice and leeks.

Spinach & Potato Galette

Creamy layers of potato, spinach and herbs make a simple, but delightful dish.

Serves 6
900g/2lb large potatoes, peeled
450g/1lb fresh spinach
2 eggs

400g/14oz/1¾ cups low-fat cream cheese
15ml/1 tbsp grainy mustard
50g/2oz chopped fresh herbs (chives, parsley, chervil or sorrel)
salt and ground black pepper
salad, to serve

1 Preheat the oven to 180°C/350°F/Gas 4. Line a deep 23cm/9in round cake tin (pan) with baking parchment.

2 Place the potatoes in a large pan and cover with cold water. Bring to the boil and cook for 10 minutes. Drain well and leave to cool slightly before slicing thinly.

3 Wash the spinach and place it in a large pan with only the water that still clings to the leaves. Cover and cook over a low heat, stirring once, until the spinach has just wilted. Drain well in a sieve and squeeze out the excess moisture with your hands. Chop finely.

4 Beat the eggs with the cream cheese and mustard, then stir in the chopped spinach and fresh herbs.

5 Place a layer of the sliced potatoes in the lined tin, arranging them in concentric circles. Top with a spoonful of the cream cheese mixture and spread out.

6 Continue layering, seasoning to taste with salt and pepper as you go, until all the potatoes and the cream cheese mixture have been used. Cover the cake tin with foil and place it in a roasting pan.

7 Fill the roasting pan with enough boiling water to come halfway up the sides of the cake tin and cook in the oven for 45–50 minutes. Turn out on to a plate and serve hot or cold, with a salad of dressed leaves and tomatoes.

Roasted Gem Squash

Gem squash has a sweet, subtle flavour that contrasts well with black olives and sun-dried tomatoes. The rice adds substance and texture.

Serves 2–4
4 whole gem squashes
225g/8oz/2 cups cooked white
   long grain rice
4 pieces sun-dried tomatoes, in
   oil, drained and chopped, plus
   30ml/2 tbsp oil from the jar
50g/2oz/ ½ cup pitted black
   olives, chopped
15ml/1 tbsp chopped fresh basil
   leaves, plus fresh basil sprigs,
   to garnish
60ml/4 tbsp soft goat's cheese
tzatziki, to serve

1 Preheat the oven to 180°C/350°F/Gas 4. Trim away the base of each squash, slice off the top, scoop out the seeds with a spoon and discard.

2 Mix together the rice, sun-dried tomatoes, olives, basil and cheese in a bowl. Stir in half the oil from the jar.

3 Use a little of the remaining oil to grease a shallow ovenproof dish that is just large enough to hold the squash side by side. Divide the rice mixture among the squash and place them in the dish. Drizzle any remaining oil over.

4 Cover with foil and bake for 45–50 minutes, until tender. Garnish with basil sprigs and serve with tzatziki.

> **Cook's Tip**
> 225g/8oz/2 cups cooked rice is the equivalent of 65g/2½oz/ generous ⅓ cup raw rice.

> **Variations**
> • If you are not keen on olives, use raisins instead.
> • If gem squashes are not available, serve half an acorn squash per person instead.

Stuffed Vegetables

Cooking for friends is fun when there are colourful dishes such as this with its interesting selection of different vegetables

Serves 4
45ml/3 tbsp olive oil, plus extra
   for greasing
1 aubergine (eggplant)
1 green (bell) pepper
2 beefsteak tomatoes
1 onion, chopped
2 garlic clove, crushed
115g/4oz/1½ cups button
   (white) mushrooms, chopped
1 carrot, grated
225g/8oz/2 cups cooked white
   long grain rice
15ml/1 tbsp chopped fresh dill
90g/3½oz/scant ½ cup
   crumbled feta cheese
75g/3oz/¾ cup pine nuts,
   lightly toasted
30ml/2 tbsp currants
salt and ground black pepper

1 Preheat the oven to 190°C/375°F/Gas 5. Lightly grease a shallow ovenproof dish. Cut the aubergine in half, through the stalk, and scoop out the flesh from each half to leave two hollow "boats". Dice the aubergine flesh. Cut the green pepper in half lengthways and remove the seeds.

2 Cut off the tops from the tomatoes and hollow out the centres. Chop the flesh and add it to the diced aubergine. Drain the tomatoes upside down on kitchen paper.

3 Bring a pan of water to the boil, add the aubergine halves and blanch for 3 minutes. Add the pepper halves and blanch for 3 minutes more. Drain, then place all the vegetables, hollow side up, in the prepared dish.

4 Heat 30ml/2 tbsp of the oil in a pan and cook the onion and garlic for about 5 minutes. Stir in the diced aubergine and tomato mixture with the mushrooms and carrot. Cover, cook for 5 minutes, until softened, then mix in the rice, dill, feta, pine nuts and currants. Season to taste with salt and pepper.

5 Divide the mixture among the vegetable shells, drizzle the remaining olive oil over and bake for 20 minutes, until the topping has browned. Serve hot or cold.

Broccoli & Chestnut Terrine

Served hot or cold, this versatile terrine is equally suitable for a dinner party or a celebration picnic.

Serves 4–6

450g/1lb broccoli, cut into small florets
225g/8oz cooked chestnuts, coarsely chopped
50g/2oz/1 cup fresh wholemeal (whole-wheat) breadcrumbs
60ml/4 tbsp low-fat natural (plain) yogurt
30ml/2 tbsp freshly grated Parmesan cheese
freshly grated nutmeg
2 eggs, beaten
salt and ground black pepper
steamed new potatoes and dressed salad leaves, to serve

1 Preheat the oven to 180°C/350°F/Gas 4. Line a 900g/2lb loaf tin (pan) with non-stick baking parchment.

2 Blanch or steam the broccoli for 3–4 minutes, until just tender. Drain well. Reserve one-quarter of the florets (choosing the smallest ones) and chop the rest finely.

3 Put the chestnuts in a bowl and stir in breadcrumbs, yogurt and Parmesan. Season with nutmeg, salt and pepper to taste, then stir in the chopped broccoli, and the beaten eggs. Fold in the reserved broccoli florets.

4 Spoon the broccoli mixture into the prepared tin and level the surface. Place the loaf tin in a roasting pan. Pour in boiling water to come halfway up the sides of the loaf tin. Bake for 20–25 minutes.

5 Remove from the oven and invert onto a plate or tray. Serve in slices, with new potatoes and dressed leaves.

> **Cook's Tip**
> To cook chestnuts, nick the shells, roast in the oven for about 5 minutes, peel and then steam or boil.

Ratatouille Pancakes

Pretty enough to serve for a dinner party and packed with juicy vegetables, these pancakes make a tasty treat.

Serves 4

75g/3oz/2/3 cup plain (all-purpose) flour
25g/1oz/1/4 cup medium oatmeal
1 egg, lightly beaten
300ml/1/2 pint/1 1/4 cups skimmed milk
light oil cooking spray, for greasing
mixed salad, to serve

For the filling

1 large aubergine (eggplant), cut into 2.5cm/1in cubes
1 garlic clove, crushed
2 medium courgettes (zucchini), sliced
1 green (bell) pepper, seeded and sliced
1 red (bell) pepper, seeded and sliced
75ml/5 tbsp vegetable stock
200g/7oz can chopped tomatoes
5ml/1 tsp cornflour (cornstarch), mixed to a paste with 10ml/2 tsp water
salt and ground black pepper

1 Sift the flour and a pinch of salt into a bowl. Stir in the oatmeal. Make a well in the centre, add the egg and half the milk and mix to a smooth batter. Gradually beat in the remaining milk. Cover the bowl and set aside for 30 minutes.

2 Spray an 18cm/7in crêpe pan with cooking spray and heat, then pour in just enough batter to cover the base. Cook for 2–3 minutes, until set and the underside is golden. Flip over and cook for 1–2 minutes more. Slide the pancake on to a plate lined with baking parchment. Make more pancakes, stacking them interleaved with baking parchment. Keep warm.

3 Put the aubergine cubes in a colander and sprinkle with salt. Leave to drain for 30 minutes. Rinse thoroughly and drain again.

4 Put the garlic, courgettes, peppers, stock and tomatoes into a large pan. Simmer, stirring occasionally, for 10 minutes. Add the aubergine and cook for 15 minutes more. Stir in the cornflour paste and simmer for 2 minutes. Season to taste. Spoon the mixture into the middle of each pancake. Fold them in half, then in half again to make cones. Serve with salad.

Penne with Artichokes

The sauce for this pasta dish is garlicky and richly flavoured. It would make the perfect first course for a dinner party during the globe artichoke season.

Serves 6
juice of ½ lemon
2 globe artichokes
15ml/1 tbsp olive oil
1 small fennel bulb, thinly sliced, with feathery tops reserved
1 onion, finely chopped
4 garlic cloves, finely chopped
a handful of fresh flat leaf parsley, coarsely chopped
400g/14oz can chopped Italian plum tomatoes
150ml/¼ pint/⅔ cup dry white wine
350g/12oz/3 cups dried penne
10ml/2 tsp capers, chopped
salt and ground black pepper
freshly grated Parmesan cheese, to serve

1 Fill a bowl with cold water and add the lemon juice. Cut off the artichoke stalks, then pull off and discard the outer leaves. Cut off the tops of the pale inner leaves so that the base remains. Cut this in half lengthways, then prise out and discard the hairy choke. Cut the artichokes lengthways into 5mm/¼in slices, adding these to the bowl of acidulated water.

2 Bring a large pan of lightly salted water to the boil, add the artichokes and boil them for 5 minutes. Drain and set aside.

3 Heat the oil in a large frying pan and cook the fennel, onion, garlic and parsley over a low heat for about 10 minutes, until the fennel has softened and is lightly coloured. Add the tomatoes and wine, with salt and pepper to taste. Bring to the boil, stirring, then simmer for 10–15 minutes. Stir in the artichokes, replace the lid and simmer for 10 minutes more.

4 Meanwhile, bring a pan of lightly salted water to the boil and cook the pasta for about 12 minutes, until it is al dente.

5 Drain the pasta and return it to the clean pan. Stir the capers into the sauce, pour it over the pasta and toss well. Serve immediately, garnished with the reserved fennel fronds. Offer grated Parmesan separately.

Conchiglie with Roasted Vegetables

Nothing could be simpler – or more delicious – than tossing freshly cooked pasta with roasted vegetables.

Serves 4
1 small aubergine (eggplant)
30ml/2 tbsp extra virgin olive oil, plus extra for brushing
1 red (bell) pepper, seeded and cut into 1cm/½in squares
1 orange (bell) pepper, seeded and cut into 1cm/½in squares
2 courgettes (zucchini), coarsely diced
15ml/1 tbsp chopped fresh flat leaf parsley
5ml/1 tsp dried oregano
250g/9oz baby Italian plum tomatoes, halved lengthways
2 garlic cloves, coarsely chopped
350g/12oz/3 cups dried conchiglie
salt and ground black pepper
4–6 fresh herb flowers, to garnish

1 Preheat the oven to 230°C/450°F/Gas 8. Cut the aubergine in half and score the cut sides deeply. Brush a roasting pan lightly with oil and place the aubergine halves on it, cut sides down. Roast for 15 minutes. Remove the aubergine from the oven and lower the temperature to 190°C/375°F/Gas 5.

2 Cut the aubergine halves into chunks and return them to the roasting pan. Add the red and orange peppers and courgettes. Pour the olive oil over the vegetables and sprinkle with the herbs and salt and pepper to taste. Stir well. Roast for about 30 minutes, stirring twice. Stir in the tomatoes and garlic, then roast for 20 minutes more, stirring once or twice.

3 Meanwhile, bring a large pan of lightly salted water to the boil and cook the pasta for about 12 minutes or until it is al dente.

4 Drain the pasta and tip it into a warmed bowl. Add the roasted vegetables and toss well. Garnish with herb flowers.

Cook's Tip
Roasting the aubergine (eggplant) first releases some of its liquid and also makes it less likely to absorb fat.

Polenta with Baked Tomatoes & Olives

A staple of northern Italy, polenta is a nourishing, filling food, served here with a delicious fresh tomato and olive topping.

Serves 4–6
2 litres/3½ pints/9 cups water
500g/1¼lb/4½ cups quick-
    cook polenta
10ml/2 tsp olive oil, plus extra
    for greasing
12 large ripe plum
    tomatoes, sliced
4 garlic cloves, thinly sliced
30ml/2 tbsp chopped fresh
    oregano or marjoram
115g/4oz/1 cup pitted
    black olives
salt and ground black pepper

1 Pour the water into a large pan and bring it to the boil. Add the polenta, whisking constantly, and continue to whisk while simmering for 5 minutes.

2 Remove the pan from the heat and pour the polenta into a 33 x 23cm/13 x 9in Swiss roll tin (jelly roll pan). Smooth the surface level and leave to cool.

3 Preheat the oven to 180°C/350°F/Gas 4. When the polenta is cool and set, stamp out 12 rounds with a 7.5cm/3in round pastry cutter. Lay them so that they overlap slightly in a lightly oiled ovenproof dish.

4 Layer the tomatoes, garlic, fresh herbs and olives on top of the polenta, seasoning the layers with salt and pepper to taste as you go. Drizzle with the olive oil and bake, uncovered, for 30–35 minutes. Serve immediately.

Cook's Tip
Olive oil contains a high proportion of monounsaturated fats – the "good" fats – as well as vitamin A. It is a healthy choice, as it helps to lower levels of blood cholesterol and forms a useful part of a low-fat diet.

Potato Gnocchi with Hazelnut Sauce

These delicate potato dumplings are dressed with a light creamy-tasting hazelnut sauce.

Serves 4
675g/1½lb large potatoes
115g/4oz/1 cup plain (all-
    purpose) flour, plus extra
    for dusting

For the hazelnut sauce
115g/4oz/1 cup
    hazelnuts, roasted
1 garlic clove, coarsely chopped
2.5ml/½ tsp grated lemon rind
2.5ml/½ tsp lemon juice
30ml/2 tbsp sunflower oil
150g/5oz/scant ¾ cup low-fat
    fromage blanc
salt and ground black pepper

1 Make the sauce. Put just over half of the hazelnuts in a food processor or blender with the garlic, grated lemon rind and juice. Process until coarsely chopped. With the motor running, gradually add the oil until the mixture is smooth. Spoon into a heatproof bowl and mix in the fromage blanc. Season to taste.

2 Put the potatoes in a pan of cold water. Bring to the boil and cook for 20–25 minutes. Drain well. When cool enough to handle, peel them and pass through a food mill into a bowl.

3 Add the flour, a little at a time, until the mixture is smooth and slightly sticky. Add salt to taste. Roll out the mixture on a floured board to a long sausage 1cm/½in in diameter. Cut into 2cm/¾in lengths. Roll one piece at a time on a floured fork to make the characteristic ridges. Flip on to a floured plate or tray.

4 Bring a large pan of water to the boil and drop in about 20 gnocchi at a time. They will rise to the surface. Cook for 10–15 seconds, then lift them out with a slotted spoon. Drop into a dish and keep hot. Continue with the rest of the gnocchi.

5 To heat the sauce, place the bowl over a pan of simmering water and heat gently, being careful not to let it curdle. Pour the sauce over the gnocchi. Coarsely chop the remaining hazelnuts, sprinkle them over the top and serve.

Wild Rice Rösti with Carrot & Orange Purée

Rösti is a traditional dish from Switzerland. This variation has the extra nuttiness of wild rice.

Serves 6
50g/2oz/ ¹/₃ cup wild rice
900g/2lb large potatoes
30ml/2 tbsp walnut oil

5ml/1 tsp yellow mustard seeds
1 onion, finely chopped
30ml/2 tbsp fresh thyme leaves
salt and ground black pepper
broccoli and green beans, to serve

For the purée
1 large orange
350g/12oz carrots, chopped

1 Make the purée. Pare two large strips of rind from the orange and put them in a pan with the carrots. Cover with cold water and bring to the boil. Cook for 10 minutes, or until the carrots are tender. Drain well and discard the rind. Squeeze the orange and put 60ml/4 tbsp of the juice in a blender or food processor with the carrots. Process to a purée.

2 Place the wild rice in a clean pan and cover with water. Bring to the boil and cook for 30–40 minutes, until the rice is just starting to split, but is still crunchy. Drain.

3 Put the unpeeled potatoes in a large pan and cover with cold water. Bring to the boil and cook for 15 minutes. Drain well. When they are cool enough to handle, peel them and grate them coarsely into a large bowl. Add the cooked rice.

4 Heat 15ml/1 tbsp of the oil in a non-stick frying pan and stir in the mustard seeds. When they start to pop, add the onion and cook gently for 5 minutes, until softened. Add to the potato mixture, then stir in the thyme leaves. Season to taste.

5 Heat the remaining oil in the frying pan and add the potato mixture. Press down well and cook for 10 minutes. Cover the pan with an inverted plate. Flip over, then slide the rösti back into the pan. Cook for 10 minutes more. Meanwhile, reheat the purée. Serve the rösti, with broccoli, beans and the purée.

Mixed Mushroom & Parmesan Risotto

A brown rice risotto of mixed mushrooms, herbs and fresh Parmesan cheese, this is beautifully moist and full of flavour.

Serves 4
10g/ ¹/₄oz/ 2 tbsp dried porcini mushrooms
150ml/ ¹/₄ pint/²/₃ cup hot water
15ml/1 tbsp olive oil
4 shallots, finely chopped

2 garlic cloves, crushed
450g/1lb/6 cups mixed cultivated and wild mushrooms, sliced
250g/9oz/1 ¹/₄ cups long grain brown rice
900ml/1 ¹/₂ pints/3³/₄ cups hot vegetable stock
45ml/3 tbsp chopped fresh flat leaf parsley
60ml/4 tbsp freshly grated Parmesan cheese
salt and ground black pepper

1 Soak the porcini mushrooms in the hot water for 20 minutes. Heat the oil in a large, heavy pan. Add the shallots and garlic and cook over a low heat, stirring occasionally, for about 5 minutes, until softened. Drain the porcini, reserving their liquid, and chop them coarsely.

2 Add all the mushrooms to the pan, with the strained porcini soaking liquid. Stir in the brown rice and one-third of the hot stock – keep the stock simmering in a pan.

3 Bring to the boil, lower the heat and simmer gently, stirring frequently, until all the liquid has been absorbed. Add a ladleful of hot stock and stir until it, too, has been absorbed.

4 Continue in this way, adding a ladleful of hot stock at a time and stirring frequently, until the rice is cooked and creamy, but still retains "bite" at the centre of the grain. This should take about 35 minutes and it may not be necessary to add all the vegetable stock.

5 Season with plenty of salt and pepper, stir in the chopped parsley and grated Parmesan and transfer to a warmed serving dish. Serve immediately.

Lentil Risotto with Vegetables

Although purists may blanch at the concept of adding lentils to a risotto, this actually works very well. The lentils benefit from soaking, but if you are in a hurry, use red split lentils, which don't need to be soaked.

Serves 4

225g/8oz/generous 1 cup
  brown basmati rice, washed
  and drained
20ml/4 tsp sunflower oil
1 large onion, thinly sliced
2 garlic cloves, crushed
1 large carrot, cut into
  thin batons
115g/4oz/ ½ cup green or brown
  lentils, soaked and drained
5ml/1 tsp ground cumin
5ml/1 tsp ground cinnamon
20 black cardamom seeds
6 cloves
600ml/1 pint/2½ cups
  vegetable stock
2 bay leaves
2 celery sticks
1 large avocado
3 plum tomatoes
salt and ground black pepper
green salad, to serve

1 Rinse the rice several times in cold water. If there is sufficient time, leave it to soak for 30 minutes in the water used for the final rinse. Drain well.

2 Heat the oil in a large, heavy pan. Add the onion, garlic and carrot and cook over a low heat, stirring occasionally, for 5–6 minutes, until the onion is softened.

3 Add the drained rice and lentils, with the spices, and cook the mixture over a low heat for 5 minutes more, stirring to prevent it from sticking to the pan.

4 Pour in the stock. Add the bay leaves and bring to the boil, then lower the heat, cover the pan and simmer for 15 minutes more, or until the liquid has been absorbed and the rice and lentils are tender.

5 Meanwhile, chop the celery into half-rounds and dice the avocado and tomatoes. Add the fresh ingredients to the rice and lentils and mix well. Season to taste. Spoon into a large serving bowl and serve immediately with a green salad.

Red Pepper Risotto

Several different types of risotto rice are available, and it is worth experimenting to find the one your family prefers. Look out for arborio, carnaroli and Vialone Nano.

Serves 6

3 large red (bell) peppers
30ml/2 tbsp olive oil
3 large garlic cloves, thinly sliced
1½ x 400g/14oz cans
  chopped tomatoes
2 bay leaves
450g/1lb/2½ cups arborio or
  other risotto rice
about 1.5 litres/2½ pints/6 cups
  hot vegetable stock
6 fresh basil leaves, torn
salt and ground black pepper

1 Put the peppers in a grill (broiler) pan and grill (broil) until the skins are charred and blistered. Put them in a bowl, cover with crumpled kitchen paper and leave for 10 minutes. Peel off the skins, then slice the flesh, discarding the cores and seeds.

2 Heat the oil in a wide, shallow pan. Add the garlic and tomatoes and cook over a low heat, stirring occasionally, for 5 minutes. Stir in the pepper slices and bay leaves and cook for 15 minutes more.

3 Stir the rice into the vegetable mixture and cook, stirring constantly, for 2 minutes, then add a ladleful of the hot stock. Cook, stirring constantly, until it has been absorbed – keep the stock simmering in a pan adjacent to the risotto.

4 Continue to add stock in this way, making sure that each addition has been absorbed before ladling in the next. When the rice is tender, season with salt and pepper to taste. Remove the pan from the heat, cover and leave to stand for 10 minutes before stirring in the basil and serving.

Variation
Both yellow and orange (bell) peppers are also suitable for this recipe, but green peppers are too acidic.

Lemon & Herb Risotto Cake

This unusual rice dish can be served as a main course with a mixed salad, or as a satisfying side dish. It's also good served cold and packs well for picnics.

Serves 4
light oil cooking spray
1 small leek, thinly sliced
600ml/1 pint/2½ cups
    vegetable stock

225g/8oz/generous 1 cup
    risotto rice
finely grated rind of 1 lemon
30ml/2 tbsp chopped fresh chives
30ml/2 tbsp chopped
    fresh parsley
75g/3oz/¾ cup grated half-fat
    mozzarella cheese
salt and ground black pepper

For the garnish
fresh flat leaf parsley sprigs
lemon wedges

1 Preheat the oven to 200°C/400°F/Gas 6. Thinly coat a 21cm/8½in loose-based round cake tin (pan) with light oil cooking spray and set aside.

2 Put the slices of leek in a large pan with 45ml/3 tbsp of the vegetable stock. Cook over a medium heat, stirring occasionally, for about 5 minutes, until softened. Add the rice and the remaining stock.

3 Bring to the boil. Lower the heat, cover the pan and simmer gently, stirring occasionally, for about 20 minutes, or until all the liquid has been absorbed.

4 Stir in the lemon rind, chives, chopped parsley and grated mozzarella and season with salt and pepper to taste. Spoon into the tin, cover with foil and bake for 30–35 minutes, or until lightly browned. Turn out and cut into slices. Serve immediately, garnished with parsley and lemon wedges.

> **Cook's Tip**
> If you cannot obtain risotto rice, use short grain rice – the type normally used for desserts – instead.

Vegetable Paella

A delicious change from the more traditional seafood- or chicken-based paella, this vegetarian version is full of flavour and includes plenty of healthy fibre.

Serves 6
1 onion, chopped
2 garlic cloves, crushed
225g/8oz leeks, sliced
3 celery sticks, chopped
1 red (bell) pepper, seeded
    and sliced
2 courgettes (zucchini), sliced
175g/6oz/2¼ cups brown cap
    (cremini) mushrooms, sliced

175g/6oz/1½ cups frozen peas
450g/1lb/2½ cups long grain
    brown rice
400g/14oz can cannellini beans,
    drained and rinsed
900ml/1½ pints/3¾ cups
    vegetable stock
60ml/4 tbsp dry white wine
a few saffron threads
225g/8oz cherry tomatoes, halved
45–60ml/3–4 tbsp chopped fresh
    mixed herbs
salt and ground black pepper
lemon wedges, whole cherry
    tomatoes and celery leaves,
    to garnish

1 Mix the onion, garlic, leeks, celery, red pepper, courgettes and mushrooms in a large, heavy pan or flameproof casserole. Add the peas, rice, cannellini beans, stock, wine and saffron. Bring to the boil over a medium heat, stirring constantly, then lower the heat and simmer, stirring occasionally, for about 35 minutes, until almost all the liquid has been absorbed and the rice is tender.

2 Stir in the tomatoes and chopped herbs, season to taste with salt and pepper and heat through for 1–2 minutes. Serve garnished with lemon wedges, tomatoes and celery leaves.

> **Cook's Tips**
> • Paella, which originated in Valencia, is not actually the name of the dish, but the heavy, two-handled, cast-iron pan in which it is traditionally cooked.
> • Long grain rice works very well in this recipe, but for a more authentic texture, try to obtain a Spanish rice, such as calasparra, or even use risotto rice.

Californian Citrus Fried Rice

As with all fried rice dishes, the important thing here is to make sure that the rice is cold. Add it after cooking all the other ingredients and stir to heat it through.

Serves 4–6

4 eggs
10ml/2 tsp Japanese rice vinegar
30ml/2 tbsp light soy sauce
about 45ml/3 tbsp groundnut (peanut) oil
50g/2oz/ 1/2 cup cashew nuts
2 garlic cloves, crushed
6 spring onions (scallions), diagonally sliced
2 small carrots, cut into thin strips
225g/8oz asparagus, each spear cut diagonally into 4 pieces
175g/6oz/2 1/4 cups button (white) mushrooms, halved
30ml/2 tbsp rice wine
30ml/2 tbsp water
450g/1lb/4 cups cooked white long grain rice
about 10ml/2 tsp sesame oil
1 pink grapefruit or orange, segmented
strips of orange rind, to garnish

For the hot dressing

5ml/1 tsp grated orange rind
30ml/2 tbsp Japanese rice wine
45ml/3 tbsp vegetarian "oyster" sauce
30ml/2 tbsp freshly squeezed pink grapefruit or orange juice
5ml/1 tsp medium chilli sauce

1 Beat the eggs with the vinegar and 10ml/2 tsp of the soy sauce. Heat 15ml/1 tbsp of the oil in a wok and cook the eggs until lightly scrambled. Transfer to a plate and set aside.

2 Add the cashew nuts to the wok and stir-fry for 1–2 minutes. Set aside. Heat the remaining oil and add the garlic and spring onions. Cook until the onions begin to soften, then add the carrots and stir-fry for 4 minutes.

3 Add the asparagus and cook for 2–3 minutes, then stir in the mushrooms and stir-fry for 1 minute. Stir in the rice wine, the remaining soy sauce and the water. Simmer for a few minutes.

4 Mix the ingredients for the dressing, then add to the wok and bring to the boil. Add the rice, scrambled eggs and cashews. Toss over a low heat for 3–4 minutes. Stir in the sesame oil and the citrus segments. Garnish with the orange rind and serve.

Provençal Rice

Colourful and bursting with flavour, this is a substantial lunch or supper dish.

Serves 3–4

2 onions
90ml/6 tbsp olive oil
175g/6oz/scant 1 cup brown long grain rice
10ml/2 tsp mustard seeds
475ml/16fl oz/2 cups vegetable stock
2 small red (bell) peppers, seeded and cut into chunks
1 small aubergine (eggplant), cut into cubes
2–3 courgettes (zucchini), sliced
about 12 cherry tomatoes
5–6 fresh basil leaves, torn
2 garlic cloves, finely chopped
60ml/4 tbsp white wine
60ml/4 tbsp passata (bottled strained tomatoes)
2 hard-boiled eggs, cut into wedges
8 stuffed green olives, sliced
15ml/1 tbsp drained and rinsed capers
butter, to taste
sea salt and ground black pepper
garlic bread, to serve

1 Preheat the oven to 200°C/400°F/Gas 6. Finely chop one onion. Heat 30ml/2 tbsp of the oil in a pan and cook the chopped onion gently until softened.

2 Add the rice and mustard seeds. Cook, stirring, for 2 minutes. Pour in the stock with a little salt. Bring to the boil, lower the heat, cover and simmer for 35 minutes, until the rice is tender.

3 Meanwhile, cut the remaining onion into wedges. Put these in a roasting pan with the peppers, aubergine, courgettes and tomatoes. Sprinkle over the basil leaves and garlic. Pour over the remaining oil and sprinkle with salt and pepper. Roast for 15–20 minutes, until the vegetables begin to char, stirring once. Reduce the oven temperature to 180°C/350°F/Gas 4.

4 Spoon the rice into an earthenware casserole. Put the roasted vegetables on top, together with any vegetable juices from the roasting pan, then pour over the wine and passata. Arrange the egg wedges on top, with the sliced olives and capers. Dot with butter, cover and cook for 15–20 minutes, until heated through. Serve with garlic bread.

Parsnips & Chickpeas in an Aromatic Paste

The sweet flavour of parsnips goes very well with the spices in this special-occasion stew.

Serves 4

200g/7oz/scant 1 cup dried
  chickpeas, soaked overnight
7 garlic cloves, finely chopped
1 small onion, chopped
5cm/2in piece of fresh root
  ginger, chopped
2 fresh green chillies, seeded and
  finely chopped
550ml/18fl oz/2½ cups water
30ml/2 tbsp groundnut
  (peanut) oil
5ml/1 tsp cumin seeds
10ml/2 tsp ground
  coriander seeds
5ml/1 tsp ground turmeric
2.5–5ml/½–1 tsp mild
  chilli powder
50g/2oz/½ cup cashew nuts,
  toasted and ground
2 tomatoes, peeled and chopped
900g/2lb parsnips, cut
  into chunks
5ml/1 tsp ground roasted
  cumin seeds
juice of 1 lime
salt and ground black pepper
fresh coriander (cilantro) leaves
  and toasted cashew nuts,
  to serve

1 Drain the chickpeas and put them in a heavy pan. Cover with cold water and bring to the boil. Boil vigorously for 10 minutes, then lower the heat and cook for 1–1½ hours, or until tender.

2 Set 10ml/2 tsp of the garlic aside. Place the remaining garlic in a food processor or blender with the onion, ginger and half the fresh chillies. Add 75ml/5 tbsp of the water and process to a smooth paste.

3 Heat the oil in a large, deep frying pan and cook the cumin seeds for 30 seconds. Stir in the coriander seeds, turmeric, chilli powder and the ground cashews.

4 Add the ginger and chilli paste and cook, stirring frequently, until the water begins to evaporate. Add the tomatoes and stir-fry until the mixture begins to turn red-brown in colour.

5 Drain the chickpeas and stir them into tomato mixture with the parsnips. Pour in the remaining water. Add 5ml/1 tsp salt and plenty of black pepper. Bring to the boil, stir well, then simmer, uncovered, for 15–20 minutes, until the parsnips are completely tender.

6 Reduce the liquid, if necessary, by boiling fiercely until the sauce is thick. Add the ground roasted cumin with lime juice to taste. Stir in the reserved garlic and chilli, and cook for a final 1–2 minutes. Sprinkle the coriander leaves and toasted cashew nuts over and serve immediately.

Cook's Tip
Dried chickpeas are used here, but they do demand some forethought as they require soaking. For an impromptu meal, use two cans of chickpeas, adding them when the parsnips have been cooking for about 5 minutes.

Aubergine & Chickpea Ragoût

The perfect dish for a winter supper party, this combines two hearty main ingredients with a blend of warming spices.

Serves 4

3 large aubergines
  (eggplant), cubed
200g/7oz/scant 1 cup dried
  chickpeas, soaked overnight
  and drained
45ml/3 tbsp olive oil
3 garlic cloves, chopped
2 large onions, chopped
2.5ml/½ tsp ground cumin
2.5ml/½ tsp ground cinnamon
2.5ml/½ tsp ground coriander
3 x 400g/14oz cans
  chopped tomatoes
salt and ground black pepper
cooked rice, to serve

For the garnish
30ml/2 tbsp olive oil
1 onion, sliced
1 garlic clove, sliced
fresh coriander (cilantro) sprigs

1 Put the aubergine cubes in a colander, sprinkling each layer with salt. Stand it in the sink for 30 minutes, then rinse very well. Drain thoroughly and pat dry with kitchen paper.

2 Put the chickpeas in a pan with enough water to cover. Bring to the boil. Boil vigorously for 10 minutes, then lower the heat and simmer for 1–1¼ hours, or until tender. Drain.

3 Heat the oil in a large, heavy pan. Add the garlic and onions and cook over a low heat, stirring occasionally, for 5 minutes, until softened.

4 Add the cumin, cinnamon and ground coriander and cook, stirring constantly, for a few seconds. Stir in the aubergine until coated with the spice mixture. Cook for 5 minutes.

5 Add the tomatoes and chickpeas and season to taste with salt and pepper. Cover and simmer for 20 minutes.

6 Make the garnish. Heat the oil in a frying pan. When it is very hot, add the sliced onion and garlic and cook, stirring frequently until golden and crisp. Serve the ragoût with rice, topped with the onion and garlic and garnished with coriander.

Red Pepper & Watercress Filo Purses

These crisp pastry purses have a delectable ricotta and vegetable filling. They are perfect for special occasion meals and dinner parties as they can be made in advance.

Makes 8

3 red (bell) peppers, halved
    and seeded
175g/6oz watercress
225g/8oz/1 cup low-fat
    ricotta cheese
blanched almonds, toasted
    and chopped
8 sheets of filo pastry, thawed
    if frozen
30ml/2 tbsp olive oil
salt and ground black pepper
frisée salad, to serve

1 Preheat the oven to 190°C/375°F/Gas 5. Place the red pepper halves, skin side up, on a grill (broiler) rack and grill (broil) until the skins have blistered and charred. Transfer to a bowl and cover with crumpled kitchen paper. Leave to cool slightly, then rub off the skins and chop the flesh coarsely.

2 Put the peppers and watercress in a food processor and pulse until coarsely chopped. Spoon into a bowl and stir in the ricotta and almonds. Season with salt and pepper to taste.

3 Working with one sheet of filo pastry at a time and keeping the others covered, cut out two 18cm/7in squares and two 5cm/2in squares from each sheet. Brush one large square with a little olive oil and top it with a second large square at an angle of 45 degrees to form a star shape.

4 Place one of the small squares in the centre of the star shape, brush lightly with oil and top with a second small square. Set this aside, covered with clear film (plastic wrap), and make more layered pastry shapes in the same way.

5 Divide the red pepper mixture among the pastries. Bring the edges of each together to form a purse shape and twist to seal. Place the purses on a lightly greased baking sheet and cook for 25–30 minutes, until golden. Serve with a frisée salad.

Cheese, Onion & Mushroom Flan

A tasty savoury flan makes great summer eating when you are dining *al fresco*.

Serves 6

175g/6oz/1½ cups wholemeal
    (whole-wheat) flour, plus extra
    for dusting
75g/3oz/6 tbsp low-fat
    soft margarine
1 onion, sliced
1 leek, sliced
175g/6oz/2¼ cups
    mushrooms, chopped
30ml/2 tbsp vegetable stock
2 eggs
150ml/¼ pint/⅔ cup
    skimmed milk
115g/4oz/⅔ cup frozen
    corn kernels
30ml/2 tbsp chopped fresh chives
15ml/1 tbsp chopped
    fresh parsley
75g/3oz/¾ cup finely
    grated reduced-fat mature
    (sharp) Cheddar cheese
salt and ground black pepper
fresh chives, to garnish

1 Sift the flour and a pinch of salt into a bowl. Add the margarine and rub in with your fingertips until the mixture resembles fine breadcrumbs, then add enough cold water to make a soft dough. Wrap and chill for 30 minutes.

2 Mix the onion, leek, mushrooms and vegetable stock in a pan. Bring to the boil, then cover and cook over a low heat for about 10 minutes, until the vegetables are just tender. Drain well and set aside.

3 Preheat the oven to 200°C/400°F/Gas 6. Roll out the pastry on a lightly floured surface and line a 20cm/8in flan tin (quiche pan). Place on a baking sheet. Using a slotted spoon, spread the vegetable mixture in the pastry case (pie shell).

4 Beat the eggs and milk together in a jug (pitcher). Add the corn, chopped chives, parsley and cheese and mix well. Season to taste with salt and pepper.

5 Pour the mixture over the vegetables. Bake for 20 minutes, then reduce the oven temperature to 180°C/350°F/Gas 4 and cook for 30 minutes more, until the filling is set and lightly browned. Garnish with chives and serve warm or cold in slices.

SIDE DISHES & SALADS

We often give little thought to accompaniments to the main course, and while lightly steamed broccoli, boiled rice or a simple salad of mixed leaves can be perfectly acceptable, it's fun to try something more exciting.

The recipes here have been inspired by world-wide cuisines, so if you are planning an ethnic theme to your meal, you have a wide choice. Stir-fried Noodles with Beansprouts would make a successful partner for both Chinese and many other Asian dishes, while Minted Couscous Castles is the natural choice to accompany a tagine. However, you do not have to limit yourself in this way – unconventional partnerships can often work beautifully.

Salads are wonderfully versatile – perfect for summer lunches and refreshing accompaniments all year round. In fact, you can also serve them as appetizers at the beginning of a meal or, as the French do, as palate cleansers after the main course. They are ideal when you are entertaining, as you can do most of the preparation in advance, freeing you to concentrate on cooking the main course and entertaining your guests.

Both the side dishes and salad recipes include some good ideas with grains. Most vegetarians are aware that the classic partnership of beans and rice provides all the proteins essential for health and they are also aware that this is the tired old image many non-vegetarians have of their diet. But most vegetarians also know quite well that these foods need not be boring, and there is ample proof here. It takes only ten extra minutes to turn plain boiled rice into tasty Tomato Rice, a dish that goes with almost everything from beans to roasted vegetables. Alternatively, there are some fabulous rice salads, as well as the ever-popular Tabbouleh and a fruity Cracked Wheat Salad with Oranges & Almonds.

Courgettes in Citrus Sauce

Courgettes are so attractive, especially the brightly coloured varieties, that their bland taste can sometimes be horribly disappointing. This piquant sauce makes sure that will not be the case here.

Serves 4
350g/12oz baby
   courgettes (zucchini)
4 spring onions (scallions),
   thinly sliced
2.5cm/1in piece of fresh root
   ginger, grated
30ml/2 tbsp cider vinegar
15ml/1 tbsp light soy sauce
5ml/1 tsp soft light brown sugar
45ml/3 tbsp vegetable stock
finely grated rind and juice of
   $\frac{1}{2}$ lemon and $\frac{1}{2}$ orange
5ml/1 tsp cornflour (cornstarch)
10ml/2 tsp water

1 Bring a pan of salted water to the boil. Add the courgettes, bring back to the boil and simmer for 3–4 minutes, until tender.

2 Meanwhile, combine the onions, ginger, vinegar, soy sauce, sugar, stock and orange and lemon juice and rind in a small pan. Bring to the boil, lower the heat and simmer for 2 minutes. Mix the cornflour to a paste with the water, then stir the paste into the sauce. Bring to the boil, stirring constantly until the sauce has thickened.

3 Drain the courgettes well and tip them into a warmed serving dish. Spoon over the hot sauce. Shake the dish gently to coat the courgettes and serve immediately.

Cook's Tip
If you can't find baby courgettes (zucchini) – about 7.5cm/3in long – use larger ones, but cook them whole so that they don't absorb too much water and become soggy. Halve them lengthways after cooking and then cut the halves into 10cm/4in lengths before coating them in the sauce.

Red Cabbage in Port & Red Wine

A sweet and sour, spicy red cabbage dish, with the added juiciness of pears and extra crunch of walnuts.

Serves 6
15ml/1 tbsp walnut oil
1 onion, sliced
2 whole star anise
5ml/1 tsp ground cinnamon
pinch of ground cloves

450g/1lb red cabbage,
   finely shredded
25g/1oz/2 tbsp soft dark
   brown sugar
45ml/3 tbsp red wine vinegar
300ml/$\frac{1}{2}$ pint/1$\frac{1}{4}$ cups red wine
150ml/$\frac{1}{4}$ pint/$\frac{2}{3}$ cup port
2 pears, cut into 1cm/$\frac{1}{2}$in cubes
115g/4oz/$\frac{2}{3}$ cup raisins
115g/4oz/1 cup walnut halves
salt and ground black pepper

1 Heat the oil in a large, heavy pan. Add the onion and cook over a low heat, stirring occasionally, for about 5 minutes, until softened but not coloured.

2 Add the star anise, cinnamon, cloves and cabbage and cook for about 3 minutes more.

3 Stir in the sugar, vinegar, red wine and port. Cover the pan and simmer gently for 10 minutes, stirring occasionally.

4 Stir in the cubed pears and raisins and cook, without replacing the lid, for 10 minutes more, or until the cabbage is tender. Season to taste with salt and pepper. Mix in the walnut halves and serve immediately.

Cook's Tip
The vinegar and wine help to preserve the beautiful colour of the cabbage as well as adding to the flavour.

Variation
Juniper berries taste wonderful with red cabbage. Omit the star anise and cinnamon and add 15ml/1 tbsp juniper berries with the ground cloves.

Roasted Mediterranean Vegetables with Pecorino

Aubergines, courgettes, peppers and tomatoes make a marvellous medley when roasted and served drizzled with fragrant olive oil. Shavings of ewe's milk pecorino add the perfect finishing touch.

Serves 4–6
1 aubergine (eggplant), sliced
2 courgettes (zucchini), sliced
2 red or yellow (bell) peppers,
  quartered and seeded
1 large onion, thickly sliced
2 large carrots, cut in batons
4 firm plum tomatoes, halved
extra virgin olive oil, for brushing
  and sprinkling
45ml/3 tbsp chopped
  fresh parsley
45ml/3 tbsp pine nuts,
  lightly toasted
115g/4oz piece of
  pecorino cheese
salt and ground black pepper

1 Layer the aubergine slices in a colander, sprinkling each layer with a little salt. Leave to drain over a sink for about 20 minutes, then rinse thoroughly under cold running water, drain well and pat dry with kitchen paper. Preheat the oven to 220°C/425°F/Gas 7.

2 Spread out the aubergine slices, courgettes, peppers, onion, carrots and tomatoes in one or two large roasting pans. Brush them lightly with olive oil and roast them for 20–30 minutes, or until they are lightly browned and the skins on the peppers have begun to blister.

3 Transfer the vegetables to a large serving platter. If you like, peel the peppers and discard the skins. Trickle over any vegetable juices from the pan and season to taste with salt and pepper. As the vegetables cool, sprinkle them with more olive oil. When they are at room temperature, mix in the fresh parsley and toasted pine nuts.

4 Using a swivel vegetable peeler, shave the pecorino and sprinkle the shavings over the vegetables.

Lemony Vegetable Parcels

What could be prettier – or more convenient – than these handy packages of winter vegetables? They're guaranteed to brighten up even the dreariest day.

Serves 4
2 medium carrots, cubed
1 small swede (rutabaga), cubed
1 large parsnip, cubed
1 leek, sliced
finely grated rind of ¹/₂ lemon
15ml/1 tbsp lemon juice
15ml/1 tbsp wholegrain mustard
5ml/1 tsp walnut or sunflower oil
salt and ground black pepper

1 Preheat the oven to 190°C/375°F/Gas 5. Place the carrot, swede and parsnip cubes in a large bowl, then add the sliced leek. Stir in the lemon rind and juice and the mustard. Season to taste with salt and pepper.

2 Cut four 30cm/12in squares of non-stick baking parchment and brush them lightly with the oil. Divide the vegetable mixture among them. Roll up the parchment from one side, then twist the ends firmly to seal.

3 Transfer the parcels to a baking sheet and bake them for 50–55 minutes, or until the vegetables are just tender.

4 Serve on heated plates, opening each parcel slightly to reveal the contents.

Cook's Tip
If you haven't got any baking parchment, use greaseproof (waxed) paper, but foil is not suitable for these parcels.

Variation
Substitute the same quantity of curry or tikka paste for the mustard and omit the lemon rind and juice.

Baked Cabbage

This healthy and economical dish uses the whole cabbage, including the flavoursome core.

Serves 4
1 green or white cabbage, about
   675g/1½lb
15ml/1 tbsp light olive oil
30ml/2 tbsp water
45–60ml/3–4 tbsp
   vegetable stock
4 firm, ripe tomatoes, peeled
   and chopped
5ml/1 tsp mild chilli powder
15ml/1 tbsp chopped fresh
   parsley or fennel, to
   garnish (optional)

For the topping
3 firm ripe tomatoes, thinly sliced
15ml/1 tbsp olive oil
salt and ground black pepper

1 Preheat the oven to 180°C/350°F/Gas 4. Shred the leaves and the core of the cabbage finely. Heat the oil in a frying pan with the water and add the cabbage. Cover and cook over a very low heat, to allow the cabbage to sweat, for 5–10 minutes. Stir occasionally.

2 Pour in the vegetable stock, then stir in the tomatoes. Cook over a low heat for a further 10 minutes. Season with the chilli powder and a little salt.

3 Tip the cabbage mixture into a large square ovenproof dish. Level the surface and arrange the sliced tomatoes on top. Brush with the oil, then sprinkle with salt and pepper to taste.

4 Bake for 30–40 minutes, or until the tomatoes are just starting to brown. Serve hot, with a little parsley or fennel sprinkled over the top, if you like.

Cook's Tips
To vary the taste, add seeded, diced red or green (bell) peppers to the cabbage with the tomatoes. If you have a shallow flameproof casserole, you could cook the cabbage in it on the hob (stovetop) and then transfer the casserole to the oven.

Broccoli & Cauliflower with Cider & Apple Mint Sauce

The cider sauce is also ideal for other vegetables, such as celery or beans.

Serves 4
15ml/1 tbsp olive oil
1 large onion, chopped
2 large carrots, chopped
1 large garlic clove
15ml/1 tbsp dill seeds
4 large fresh apple mint sprigs
30ml/2 tbsp plain (all-
   purpose) flour
300ml/½ pint/1¼ cups dry cider
500g/1¼ lb/4 cups broccoli florets
500g/1¼lb/4 cups
   cauliflower florets
30ml/2 tbsp tamari
10ml/2 tsp mint jelly
salt

1 Heat the olive oil in a large, heavy frying pan. Add the onion, carrots, garlic, dill seeds and apple mint leaves and cook over a low heat, stirring occasionally, for about 5 minutes, until the vegetables are soft.

2 Stir in the flour and cook, stirring constantly, for 1 minute, then stir in the cider. Bring to the boil, then simmer until the sauce looks glossy. Remove the pan from the heat and set aside to cool slightly.

3 Bring two small pans of lightly salted water to the boil and cook the broccoli and cauliflower separately until just tender.

4 Meanwhile, pour the sauce into a food processor and add the tamari and mint jelly. Process to a fine purée.

5 Drain the broccoli and cauliflower well and mix them in a warmed serving dish. Pour over the sauce, mix lightly to coat and serve immediately.

Cook's Tip
Tamari is a Japanese soy sauce. It is dark and thick and tastes less salty than Chinese soy.

Tomato Rice

Proof positive that you don't need elaborate ingredients or complicated cooking methods to make a delicious dish.

Serves 4
400g/14oz/2 cups basmati rice
30ml/2 tbsp sunflower oil
2.5ml/ ½ tsp onion seeds
1 onion, sliced
2 tomatoes, chopped

1 orange or yellow (bell) pepper,
   seeded and sliced
5ml/1 tsp crushed fresh
   root ginger
1 garlic clove, crushed
5ml/1 tsp hot chilli powder
1 potato, diced
7.5ml/1½ tsp salt
750ml/1¼ pints/3 cups water
30–45ml/2–3 tbsp chopped
   fresh coriander (cilantro)

1 Rinse the rice several times in cold water. If there is sufficient time, leave it to soak for about 30 minutes in the water used for the final rinse.

2 Heat the oil in a large, heavy pan and cook the onion seeds for about 30 seconds, until they are giving off their aroma. Add the sliced onion and cook over a low heat, stirring occasionally, for 5 minutes, then increase the heat slightly.

3 Stir in the tomatoes, orange or yellow pepper, ginger, garlic, chilli powder, diced potato and salt. Stir-fry over a medium heat for about 5 minutes more.

4 Drain the rice thoroughly. Add it to the pan, then stir for about 1 minute until the grains are well coated in the spicy vegetable mixture.

5 Pour in the measured water and bring it to the boil, then lower the heat, cover the pan with a tight-fitting lid and cook the rice for 12–15 minutes. Remove from the heat, without lifting the lid, and leave the rice to stand for 5 minutes.

6 Gently fork through the rice to fluff up the grains, stir in the chopped coriander and transfer to a warmed serving dish. Serve immediately.

Wild Rice Pilaff

Wild rice isn't a rice at all, but is actually a type of wild grass. Call it what you will, it has a wonderful nutty flavour and makes a fine addition to this fruity, Middle-Eastern mixture.

Serves 6
200g/7oz/1 cup wild rice
40g/1½oz/3 tbsp butter
½ onion, finely chopped

200g/7oz/1 cup long
   grain rice
475ml/16fl oz/2 cups
   vegetable stock
75g/3oz/ ¾ cup flaked
   (sliced) almonds
115g/4oz/ ⅔ cup sultanas
   (golden raisins)
30ml/2 tbsp chopped
   fresh parsley
salt and ground black pepper

1 Bring a large pan of lightly salted water to the boil. Add the wild rice and 5ml/1 tsp salt. Lower the heat, cover and simmer gently for 45–60 minutes, until the rice is tender. Drain well.

2 Meanwhile, melt 15g/ ½oz/1 tbsp of the butter in another pan and cook the onion until it is just softened. Stir in the long grain rice and cook for 1 minute more.

3 Stir in the stock and bring to the boil. Lower the heat, cover tightly and simmer gently for about 30 minutes, until the rice is tender and the liquid has been absorbed.

4 Melt the remaining butter in a small pan. Add the almonds and cook until they are just golden. Set aside.

5 Tip both types of rice into a warmed serving dish and stir in the almonds, sultanas and half the parsley. Adjust the seasoning if necessary. Sprinkle with the remaining parsley and serve.

Cook's Tip
Like all pilaff dishes, this one must be made with well-flavoured stock. Make your own, if possible, and let it reduce so that the flavour intensifies.

Minted Couscous Castles

These pretty little timbales are perfect for serving as part of a summer lunch. They're virtually fat-free, so you can indulge yourself with impunity.

Makes 4
225g/8oz/1¼ cups couscous
475ml/16fl oz/2 cups boiling
   vegetable stock
15ml/1 tbsp lemon juice
2 tomatoes, diced
30ml/2 tbsp chopped fresh mint
vegetable oil, for brushing
salt and ground black pepper
fresh mint sprigs, to garnish

1 Put the couscous in a bowl and pour over the boiling stock. Cover and leave to stand for 30 minutes, until all the stock has been absorbed and the grains are tender.

2 Stir in the lemon juice with the tomatoes and chopped mint. Season to taste with salt and pepper.

3 Brush the insides of four cups or individual moulds lightly with oil. Spoon in the couscous mixture and pack down firmly. Chill for several hours.

4 Invert the castles on a platter and serve cold, garnished with mint. Alternatively, cover and heat gently in a low oven, then turn out and serve hot.

Cook's Tip
Moroccan couscous, the kind most commonly seen in Western supermarkets, is produced in fairly small grains, whereas the grains of Israeli couscous are about the size of peppercorns, and Lebanese couscous resembles small chickpeas in appearance. All three types may be cooked in the slow, traditional manner. Only Moroccan couscous is produced in an "instant", ready-cooked form, but this is not immediately distinguishable from traditional couscous, so always check the instructions on the packet.

Stir-fried Noodles with Beansprouts

A classic Chinese noodle dish that makes a marvellous accompaniment. In China, noodles are served at virtually every meal – even breakfast.

Serves 4
175g/6oz dried egg noodles
15ml/1 tbsp vegetable oil
1 garlic clove, finely chopped

1 small onion, halved and sliced
225g/8oz/2 cups beansprouts
1 small red (bell) pepper, seeded
   and cut into strips
1 small green (bell) pepper,
   seeded and cut into strips
2.5ml/½ tsp salt
1.5ml/¼ tsp ground
   white pepper
30ml/2 tbsp light soy sauce

1 Bring a large pan of water to the boil. Add the noodles and remove the pan from the heat. Cover and leave to stand for about 4 minutes, until the noodles are just tender.

2 Heat the oil in a wok. When it is very hot, add the garlic, stir briefly, then add the onion slices. Cook, stirring, for 1 minute, then add the beansprouts and peppers. Stir-fry for 2–3 minutes.

3 Drain the noodles thoroughly, then add them to the wok. Toss over the heat, using two spatulas or wooden spoons, for 2–3 minutes, or until the ingredients are well mixed and have heated through.

4 Add the salt, white pepper and soy sauce and stir thoroughly before serving the noodle mixture in heated bowls.

Variations
This is a useful, basic noodle dish that not only makes a good accompaniment, but can also be easily adapted to make a more substantial main course. For example, add carrot batons, quartered button (white) mushrooms and mangetouts (snow peas) with the beansprouts in step 2, or ½ cucumber, cut into batons, with the vegetables in step 2 and 115g/4oz/2 cups shredded spinach just before adding the noodles in step 3.

Caesar Salad

There are few dishes more famous than this popular combination of crisp lettuce leaves and Parmesan in a fresh egg dressing.

Serves 4
2 large garlic cloves, halved
45ml/3 tbsp extra virgin olive oil
4 slices wholemeal (whole-wheat) bread
1 small cos or romaine lettuce
50g/2oz piece of Parmesan cheese, shaved or coarsely grated

For the dressing
1 egg
10ml/2 tsp French mustard
5ml/1 tsp vegetarian Worcestershire sauce
30ml/2 tbsp fresh lemon juice
30ml/2 tbsp extra virgin olive oil
salt and ground black pepper

1 Preheat the oven to 190°C/375°F/Gas 5. Rub the inside of a salad bowl with one of the half cloves of garlic.

2 Heat the oil gently with the remaining garlic in a frying pan for 5 minutes, then remove and discard the garlic.

3 Remove the crusts from the bread and cut the crumb into small cubes. Toss these in the garlic-flavoured oil, making sure that they are well coated. Spread out the bread cubes on a baking sheet, and bake for about 10 minutes, until crisp. Remove from the oven, then leave to cool.

4 Separate the lettuce leaves, wash and dry them and arrange in a shallow salad bowl. Chill until ready to serve.

5 Make the dressing. Bring a small pan of water to the boil, lower the egg into the water and boil for 1 minute only. Crack it into a bowl. Use a teaspoon to scoop out and discard any softly set egg white. Using a balloon whisk, beat in the French mustard, Worcestershire sauce, lemon juice and olive oil, then season with salt and pepper to taste.

6 Sprinkle the Parmesan over the salad and then drizzle the dressing over. Sprinkle with the croûtons. Take the salad to the table, toss lightly and serve immediately.

Mixed Leaf & Herb Salad with Toasted Seeds

This salad is the perfect antidote to a rich meal as it contains fresh herbs that can aid the digestion.

Serves 4
115g/4oz/4 cups mixed salad leaves
50g/2oz/2 cups mixed salad herbs, such as coriander (cilantro), parsley, basil and rocket (arugula)
25g/1oz/2 tbsp pumpkin seeds
25g/1oz/2 tbsp sunflower seeds

For the dressing
60ml/4 tbsp extra virgin olive oil
15ml/1 tbsp balsamic vinegar
2.5ml/ ½ tsp Dijon mustard
salt and ground black pepper

1 Start by making the dressing. Combine the olive oil, balsamic vinegar and mustard in a screw-top jar. Add salt and pepper to taste. Close the jar tightly, then shake the dressing vigorously until well combined.

2 Mix the salad and herb leaves in a large bowl.

3 Toast the pumpkin and sunflower seeds in a dry frying pan over a medium heat for 2 minutes, until golden, tossing frequently to prevent them from burning. Leave the seeds to cool slightly before sprinkling them over the salad.

4 Pour the dressing over the salad and toss gently with your hands until the leaves are well coated. Serve immediately.

> **Variations**
> • Balsamic vinegar adds a rich, sweet taste to the dressing, but red or white wine vinegar could be used instead.
> • A few nasturtium flowers would look very pretty in this salad, as would borage flowers.
> • Substitute your favourite seeds for those given here.

Fruit & Nut Coleslaw

A delicious and nutritious mixture of crunchy vegetables, fruit and nuts, tossed together in a mayonnaise dressing.

Serves 6

225g/8oz white cabbage
1 large carrot
175g/6oz/ ¾ cup ready-to-eat dried apricots
50g/2oz/ ½ cup walnuts
50g/2oz/ ½ cup hazelnuts
115g/4oz/ ⅔ cup raisins
30ml/2 tbsp chopped fresh parsley
105ml/7 tbsp light mayonnaise
75ml/5 tbsp natural (plain) yogurt
salt and ground black pepper
fresh chives, to garnish

1 Finely shred the cabbage, coarsely grate the carrot and place both in a large mixing bowl.

2 Coarsely chop the dried apricots, walnuts and hazelnuts. Stir them into the cabbage and carrot mixture with the raisins and chopped parsley.

3 In a separate bowl, mix together the mayonnaise and yogurt and season to taste with salt and pepper.

4 Add the mayonnaise mixture to the cabbage mixture and toss together to mix. Cover and set aside in a cool place for at least 30 minutes before serving, to allow the flavours to mingle. Garnish with a few fresh chives and serve.

Variations
• *For a salad that is lower in fat, use low-fat natural (plain) yogurt and reduced-calorie mayonnaise.*
• *Instead of walnuts and hazelnuts, use flaked (sliced) almonds and chopped pistachios.*
• *Omit the dried apricots and add a cored and chopped, unpeeled eating apple.*
• *Substitute other dried fruit or a mixture for the apricots — try nectarines, peaches or prunes.*

Panzanella

Open-textured, Italian-style bread is essential for this colourful Tuscan salad.

Serves 6

10 thick slices day-old Italian style bread, about 275g/10oz
1 cucumber, peeled and cut into chunks
5 tomatoes, seeded and diced
1 large red onion, chopped
175g/6oz/1½ cups pitted black or green olives
20 fresh basil leaves, torn

For the dressing
60ml/4 tbsp extra virgin olive oil
15ml/1 tbsp red or white wine vinegar
salt and ground black pepper

1 Soak the bread in water to cover for about 2 minutes, then lift it out and squeeze gently, first with your hands and then in a dishtowel to remove any excess water.

2 Make the dressing. Place the oil, vinegar and seasoning in a screw-top jar. Close the lid tightly and shake vigorously. Mix the cucumber, tomatoes, onion and olives in a bowl.

3 Break the bread into chunks and add to the bowl with the basil. Pour the dressing over the salad, and toss before serving.

Date, Orange & Carrot Salad

A simple oil-free dressing is perfect on this juicy salad.

Serves 4

1 Little Gem (Bibb) lettuce
2 carrots, finely grated
2 oranges, segmented
115g/4oz/⅔ cup fresh dates, pitted and sliced lengthways
30ml/2 tbsp toasted almonds
30ml/2 tbsp lemon juice
5ml/1 tsp caster (superfine) sugar
1.5ml/¼ tsp salt
15ml/1 tbsp orange flower water

1 Spread out the lettuce leaves on a platter. Place the carrots in the centre. Surround with the oranges, dates and almonds.
2 Mix the lemon juice, sugar, salt and orange flower water. Sprinkle over the salad and serve chilled.

Grated Beetroot & Celery Salad

Raw beetroot has a lovely crunchy texture. In this Russian salad, its flavour is brought out by marinating it in a cider dressing.

Serves 4–6
450g/1lb uncooked beetroot
  (beet), peeled and grated
4 celery sticks, finely chopped
30ml/2 tbsp apple juice
fresh herbs, to garnish

For the dressing
15ml/1 tbsp cider vinegar
4 spring onions (scallions), sliced
30ml/2 tbsp chopped
  fresh parsley
45ml/3 tbsp sunflower oil
salt and ground black pepper

1 Toss the beetroot and celery with the apple juice in a bowl until well mixed.

2 Make the dressing. Put the vinegar, spring onions and parsley in a small bowl and whisk in the oil until well blended. Season with salt and pepper to taste, then stir half the dressing into the beetroot mixture.

3 Drizzle the remaining dressing over the salad, cover it and chill for 2 hours. Garnish with fresh herbs and serve.

Beetroot & Orange Salad

This is a classic combination for a refreshing salad.

Serves 4
1 small lettuce, shredded
8 cooked baby beetroot
  (beets), halved
2 oranges, peeled and segmented
30ml/2 tbsp orange juice
15ml/1 tbsp lemon juice
30ml/2 tbsp olive oil
5ml/1 tsp sugar
10ml/2 tsp chopped fresh chives,
  plus extra to garnish

1 Place the lettuce on a serving plate and top with the beetroot and orange segments in a circle.
2 Whisk together the remaining ingredients and pour over the salad. Garnish with extra chives and serve.

Fennel, Orange & Rocket Salad

This light and refreshing salad is ideal for serving with spicy or rich foods.

Serves 4
2 oranges
1 fennel bulb
115g/4oz rocket (arugula) leaves
50g/2oz/ ½ cup pitted
  black olives

For the dressing
15ml/1 tbsp balsamic vinegar
1 small garlic clove, crushed
30ml/2 tbsp extra virgin
  olive oil
salt and ground black pepper

1 With a vegetable peeler, cut thin strips of rind from the oranges, leaving the pith behind. Cut the pieces into thin strips. Set them aside.

2 Peel the oranges, removing all the white pith. Slice them into thin rounds and discard any pips (seeds). Bring a small pan of water to the boil, add the strips of rind and cook for 2–3 minutes. Drain and dry on kitchen paper.

3 Cut the fennel bulb in half lengthways and slice across the bulb as thinly as possible, preferably in a food processor fitted with a slicing disc, or using a mandoline.

4 Combine the orange rounds and fennel slices in a serving bowl and toss with the rocket leaves.

5 Make the dressing. Mix the vinegar and garlic in a bowl. Whisk in the oil, then season with salt and pepper to taste. Pour the dressing over the salad, toss well and leave to stand for a few minutes. Sprinkle with the black olives and garnish with the blanched strips of orange rind before serving.

> **Cook's Tip**
> *Although extra virgin olive oil is expensive, it is worth investing in it for salad dressings, as it has by far the best flavour.*

Romanian Pepper Salad

Try to locate authentic long sweet peppers for this salad.

Serves 4
8 long green and/or orange (bell) peppers, halved and seeded
1 garlic clove, crushed
60ml/4 tbsp wine vinegar
75ml/5 tbsp olive oil
4 tomatoes, sliced
1 red onion, thinly sliced
salt and ground black pepper
fresh coriander (cilantro) sprigs, to garnish
black bread, to serve

1 Place the pepper halves, skin side up, on a rack and grill (broil) until the skins have blistered and charred. Transfer to a bowl and cover with crumpled kitchen paper. Leave to cool slightly, then peel and cut each piece in half lengthways.

2 Mix the garlic and vinegar in a bowl, then whisk in the olive oil. Arrange the peppers, tomatoes and onion on four serving plates and pour over the garlic dressing. Season to taste, garnish with fresh coriander sprigs and serve with black bread.

Simple Pepper Salad

Peppers are perfect for making refreshing salads.

Serves 4
4 large mixed (bell) peppers, halved and seeded
60ml/4 tbsp olive oil
1 medium onion, thinly sliced
2 garlic cloves, crushed
4 tomatoes, peeled and chopped
pinch of sugar
5ml/1 tsp lemon juice
salt and ground black pepper

1 Place the peppers, skin side up, on a rack and grill (broil) until blistered. Transfer to a bowl and cover with crumpled kitchen paper. Cool slightly, then rub off the skins and slice thinly.
2 Heat the oil and cook the onion and garlic until softened. Add the peppers and tomatoes and cook for 10 minutes more.
3 Remove from the heat, stir in the sugar and lemon juice and season. Leave to cool and serve at room temperature.

Cucumber & Tomato Salad

Yogurt cools the dressing for this salad; fresh chilli hots it up. The combination works very well and is delicious with fresh bread.

Serves 4
450g/1lb firm ripe tomatoes
1/2 cucumber
1 onion
1 small hot chilli, seeded and chopped and chopped chives, to garnish
country bread or tomato toasts (see Cook's Tip), to serve

For the dressing
60ml/4 tbsp olive oil
90ml/6 tbsp thick Greek (US strained plain) yogurt
30ml/2 tbsp chopped fresh parsley or chopped chives
2.5ml/ 1/2 tsp white wine vinegar
salt and ground black pepper

1 Peel the tomatoes by first cutting a cross in the base of each tomato. Place in a bowl and cover with boiling water for 1–2 minutes, or until the skin starts to curl back from the crosses. Drain, plunge into cold water and drain again. Peel, cut the tomatoes into quarters, seed and chop.

2 Chop the cucumber and onion into pieces that are the same size as the tomatoes and put them all in a bowl.

3 Make the dressing. Whisk together the oil, yogurt, parsley or chives and vinegar in a bowl and season to taste with salt and pepper. Pour over the salad and toss all the ingredients together. Sprinkle over black pepper and the chopped chilli and chives to garnish. Serve with crusty bread or tomato toasts.

Cook's Tip
To make tomato toasts, cut a French loaf diagonally into thin slices. Mix together a crushed garlic clove, a peeled and chopped tomato and 30ml/2 tbsp olive oil. Season. Spread on the bread and bake at 220°C/425°F/Gas 7 for 10 minutes.

Tabbouleh

The classic bulgur wheat salad, this remains a winner. Serve it with roasted Mediterranean vegetables.

Serves 4

150g/5oz/scant 1 cup
  bulgur wheat
600ml/1 pint/2½ cups water
3 spring onions (scallions), finely
  chopped
2 large garlic cloves, crushed
4 firm tomatoes, peeled
  and chopped
90ml/6 tbsp chopped
  fresh parsley
60ml/4 tbsp chopped
  fresh mint
90ml/6 tbsp fresh lemon juice
75ml/5 tbsp extra virgin
  olive oil
salt and ground black pepper

1 Place the bulgur wheat in a bowl and pour over the measured water. Leave to soak for 20 minutes.

2 Line a colander with a clean dishtowel. Tip the soaked bulgur wheat into the centre, let it drain, then gather up the sides of the dishtowel and squeeze out any remaining liquid. Tip the bulgur wheat into a large bowl.

3 Add the spring onions, garlic, tomatoes, parsley and mint. Mix well, then pour over the lemon juice and olive oil. Season well, then toss so that all the ingredients are combined. Cover and chill in the refrigerator for several hours before serving.

Ratatouille

Wonderfully versatile, ratatouille can be served hot or cold. Apart from being a good side dish, it makes an excellent filling for baked potatoes and warm tortillas and a good sauce for pasta.

Serves 4–6

60ml/4 tbsp olive oil
2 large onions, chopped
2 garlic cloves, crushed
2 large aubergines (eggplant), cut
  into large cubes
3 courgettes (zucchini), sliced
2 (bell) peppers (red and green),
  seeded and sliced
3 large tomatoes, peeled, seeded
  and chopped
15ml/1 tbsp sun-dried tomato
  paste dissolved in 30ml/2 tbsp
  boiling water
30ml/2 tbsp chopped fresh
  coriander (cilantro)
salt and ground black pepper

1 Heat the oil in a large pan and cook the onions and garlic until softened. Add the aubergines and cook for 10 minutes, stirring frequently. Stir in the courgettes, peppers and tomatoes, with the diluted tomato paste and plenty of salt and pepper.

2 Bring to the boil, then lower the heat and simmer for about 30 minutes, stirring occasionally and adding a little water if needed, until the vegetables are just tender. Stir in the coriander and serve hot or cold.

Cracked Wheat Salad with Oranges & Almonds

The citrus flavours of lemon and orange really come through in this tasty salad, which can be made several hours before serving.

Serves 4

150g/5oz/scant 1 cup
  bulgur wheat
600ml/1 pint/2½ cups water
1 small green (bell) pepper,
  seeded and diced
¼ cucumber, diced
15g/½oz/½ cup chopped
  fresh mint
60ml/4 tbsp flaked (sliced)
  almonds, toasted
grated rind and juice of 1 lemon
2 seedless oranges
salt and ground black pepper
fresh mint sprigs, to garnish

1 Place the bulgur wheat in a bowl, pour over the measured water and leave to soak for 20 minutes.

2 Line a colander with a clean dishtowel. Tip the soaked bulgur wheat into the centre, let it drain, then gather up the sides of the dish towel and squeeze out any remaining liquid. Tip the bulgur wheat into a large bowl.

3 Add the green pepper, diced cucumber, mint, toasted almonds and grated lemon rind. Pour in the lemon juice and then toss thoroughly to mix.

4 Cut the rind from the oranges, then, working over a bowl to catch the juice, cut both oranges into neat segments. Add the segments and the juice to the bulgur mixture, then season to taste with salt and pepper and toss lightly. Garnish with the mint sprigs and serve.

> **Cook's Tip**
> If you have time, salt the aubergine cubes in a colander over the sink for 20 minutes. Rinse well and pat dry before using.

> **Cook's Tip**
> Bulgur is also known as cracked wheat because the grains are cracked after hulling and steaming and before drying.

Spanish Rice Salad

Ribbons of green and yellow pepper add colour and flavour to this simple salad.

Serves 6

275g/10oz/1½ cups white long grain rice
1 bunch spring onions (scallions), thinly sliced
1 green (bell) pepper, seeded and sliced
1 yellow (bell) pepper, seeded and sliced
3 tomatoes, peeled, seeded and chopped
30ml/2 tbsp chopped fresh coriander (cilantro)

For the dressing

45ml/3 tbsp mixed sunflower and olive oil
15ml/1 tbsp rice vinegar
5ml/1 tsp Dijon mustard
salt and ground black pepper

1 Bring a large pan of lightly salted water to the boil and cook the rice for 10–12 minutes, until tender but still slightly firm at the centre of the grain. Do not overcook. Drain, rinse under cold water and drain again. Leave until cold.

2 Place the rice in a large serving bowl. Add the spring onions, green and yellow peppers, tomatoes and coriander.

3 Make the dressing. Mix the oils, vinegar and mustard in a jar with a tight-fitting lid and season to taste with salt and pepper. Shake vigorously. Stir 60–75ml/4–5 tbsp of the dressing into the rice and adjust the seasoning, if necessary.

4 Cover and chill for about 1 hour before serving. Offer the remaining dressing separately.

Variations
• Cooked garden peas, cooked diced carrot and drained, canned corn can be added to this versatile salad.
• This recipe works well with long grain rice, but if you can obtain Spanish rice, it will be more authentic. This has a rounder grain, a little like risotto rice.

Fruity Brown Rice Salad

An Asian-style dressing gives this colourful rice salad extra piquancy.

Serves 4–6

115g/4oz/⅔ cup brown rice
1 small red (bell) pepper, seeded and diced
200g/7oz can corn, drained
45ml/3 tbsp sultanas (golden raisins)
225g/8oz can pineapple pieces in fruit juice
15ml/1 tbsp light soy sauce
15ml/1 tbsp sunflower oil
15ml/1 tbsp hazelnut oil
1 garlic clove, crushed
5ml/1 tsp finely chopped fresh root ginger
salt and ground black pepper
4 spring onions (scallions), diagonally sliced, to garnish

1 Bring a large pan of lightly salted water to the boil and cook the brown rice for about 30 minutes, or until it is just tender. Drain thoroughly, rinse under cold water and drain again. Set aside to cool.

2 Tip the rice into a bowl and add the red pepper, corn and sultanas. Drain the pineapple pieces, reserving the juice, then add them to the rice mixture and toss lightly.

3 Pour the reserved pineapple juice into a clean screw-top jar. Add the soy sauce, sunflower and hazelnut oils, garlic and chopped root ginger and season to taste with salt and pepper. Close the jar tightly and shake vigorously.

4 Pour the dressing over the salad and toss well. Sprinkle the spring onions over the top and serve.

Cook's Tips
• Hazelnut oil gives a distinctive flavour to any salad dressing and is especially good for leafy salads that need a bit of a lift. It is like olive oil, in that it contains mainly monounsaturated fats.
• Brown rice is often mistakenly called wholegrain. In fact, the outer husk is completely inedible and is removed from all rice, but the bran layer is left intact on brown rice.

Japanese Salad

Delicate and refreshing, this is based on a mild-flavoured, sweet-tasting seaweed, combined with radishes, cucumber and beansprouts.

Serves 4
15g/½oz/ ½ cup dried hijiki
250g/9oz/1¼ cups radishes,
 sliced into very thin rounds
1 small cucumber, cut into
 thin sticks
75g/3oz/¾ cup beansprouts

For the dressing
15ml/1 tbsp sunflower oil
15ml/1 tbsp toasted sesame oil
5ml/1 tsp light soy sauce
30ml/2 tbsp rice vinegar or
 15ml/1 tbsp wine vinegar
15ml/1 tbsp mirin or dry sherry

1 Place the hijiki in a bowl and add cold water to cover. Soak for 10–15 minutes, until it is rehydrated, then drain, rinse under cold running water and drain again. It should have almost trebled in volume.

2 Place the hijiki in a pan of water. Bring to the boil, then lower the heat and simmer for about 30 minutes, or until tender. Drain well.

3 Meanwhile, make the dressing. Place the sunflower and sesame oils, soy sauce, vinegar and mirin or sherry in a screw-top jar. Shake vigorously to combine.

4 Arrange the hijiki in a shallow bowl or platter with the radishes, cucumber and beansprouts. Pour over the dressing and toss lightly.

> **Cook's Tip**
> *Hijiki is a type of seaweed. A rich source of minerals, it comes from Japan, where it has a distinguished reputation for enhancing beauty and adding lustre to hair. Look for hijiki in Asian food stores.*

Sesame Noodle Salad

Toasted sesame oil adds a nutty flavour to this salad, which is at its best when served warm.

Serves 2–4
250g/9oz medium egg noodles
200g/7oz/1¾ cups sugar snap
 peas or mangetouts (snow
 peas), sliced diagonally
2 carrots, cut into thin strips
2 tomatoes, seeded
 and diced
30ml/2 tbsp chopped fresh
 coriander (cilantro), plus
 coriander sprigs, to garnish

15ml/1 tbsp sesame seeds
3 spring onions
 (scallions), shredded

For the dressing
10ml/2 tsp light soy sauce
30ml/2 tbsp toasted sesame
 seed oil
15ml/1 tbsp sunflower oil
4cm/1½in piece of fresh root
 ginger, finely grated
1 garlic clove, crushed

1 Bring a large pan of water to the boil, add the noodles and remove the pan from the heat. Cover and leave to stand for about 4 minutes, until the noodles are just tender.

2 Meanwhile, bring a second, smaller pan of water to the boil. Add the sugar snap peas or mangetouts, bring the water back to the boil and cook for 2 minutes. Drain and refresh under cold water, then drain again.

3 Make the dressing. Put the soy sauce, sesame seed and sunflower oils, ginger and garlic in a screw-top jar. Close tightly and shake vigorously to mix.

4 Drain the noodles thoroughly and tip them into a large bowl. Add the sugar snaps or mangetouts, carrots, tomatoes and coriander. Pour the dressing over the top and toss thoroughly with your hands to combine.

5 Sprinkle the salad with the sesame seeds, top with the shredded spring onions and coriander sprigs and serve while the noodles are still warm.

Vegetarian Ingredients

The cardinal rule when shopping for vegetarian ingredients is to choose the freshest possible produce, buying little and often. For dried goods, find a supplier with a healthy turnover, so stocks don't have time to get stale. Keep a constant lookout for new and exciting products. Vegetarian food is a growth market, and the range of available foods is constantly increasing. Once the preserve of the health-food store, vegetarian ingredients are now stocked in every supermarket, and the demand for organic produce, and products made from organic ingredients, is huge.

Vegetables & Fruit

Buy the bulk of your produce from local growers, if possible, balancing home-grown vegetables and fruit with exotic imports. Some supermarkets support local growers, including organic ones, so look out for labels that state the provenance of the produce. Several organic farms offer box schemes, where you opt to buy a box of vegetables and/or fruit every week. What goes into the box depends on what is being harvested at the time, and because everything is picked to order, it is beautifully fresh. This is a great way of buying greens such as spinach or Swiss chard. Farmer's markets are excellent sources of fruit and vegetables, as are farm stores, where growers sell their surplus. If you live in the country, look out for roadside stalls. Gardeners often grow vegetables not generally available in the shops, such as the more unusual types of squash, and sell them at very reasonable prices. Pick-your-own vegetable farms aren't so common as those offering pick-your-own fruit, but corn cobs are sometimes sold that way. Don't forget essential aromatics such as fresh garlic and root ginger.

tomatoes

apples

Swiss chard

winter squash

garlic

aubergines (eggplant)

Herbs & Spices

The most satisfying way to obtain herbs is from your own garden. You don't need acres of space as even a window-box or a few pots on the patio will yield a generous harvest. Obvious candidates are mint and parsley, preferably the flat leaf variety, but you should also aim to grow thyme, basil, sage and oregano or marjoram. If you possibly can, add coriander (cilantro), chives, chervil, rosemary and bay, all of which feature in this book. Alternatively, buy herbs from the supermarket, but use them as soon as possible after purchase. Dried herbs lose their potency quite quickly, so buy small amounts at a time, keep them in a cool, dry place (out of direct sunlight) and replace them as soon as they start to go stale.

For the best flavour, buy whole spices and seeds, and grind them as needed in a spice mill or coffee grinder kept for the purpose. Dry-frying spices before grinding intensifies their flavour. Essential spices include cardamom pods, cumin and coriander seeds, cinnamon sticks, nutmeg, dried chillies and chilli powder, cayenne, paprika, Chinese five-spice powder, garam masala, saffron, turmeric and curry powder.

flat leaf parsley

basil

cinnamon

chives and bay leaves

coriander seeds and coriander (cilantro) leaves

Clockwise from top: celery seeds, chilli powder, chilli flakes and cayenne

Grains, Pasta & Pulses

The dried versions of these easy-to-use ingredients are store-cupboard (pantry) staples. Rice is invaluable to the vegetarian cook, both as a base for vegetable stews and sautés and for stuffed vegetables. In addition to regular white and brown long grain rice, try basmati, which has a wonderful fragrance and flavour. Rinse it well before use and, if there is time, soak it in the water used for the final rinse. For risotto you will need a short grain rice, such as arborio, carnaroli or Vialone Nano. Bulgur wheat has already been partially prepared, so needs only a brief soaking before use. It is the basis for tabbouleh, and also tastes good in pilaffs and bakes. Another really useful

rice

dried pasta

lentils

grain that needs very little preparation is couscous, which is made from coarse semolina.

Dried pasta comes in an astonishing array of shapes. Some of the more unusual types are introduced in recipes in this book, but you can always substitute whatever you have in the cupboard. Dried egg noodles are essential for many Asian dishes.

Fresh pasta is becoming widely available. Find a reliable source and buy it as needed.

Pulses, such as dried beans, chickpeas, split peas and lentils, keep well and play a vital role in vegetarian cooking, as they are such a good source of many essential proteins. Most pulses need to be soaked overnight, so remember to take the time into account when you are planning your menu.

dried beans

From the Refrigerator & Freezer

Dairy products provide lacto-vegetarians (those who eat dairy produce) with valuable protein, calcium and vitamins B_{12}, A and D, but can be high in fat. Like eggs, they should be eaten in moderation. Look out for vegetarian versions of your favourite cheeses (produced with vegetable rennet). Yogurt, crème fraîche and fromage frais (farmer's cheese) are also very useful, as is tofu, a protein-rich food made from soya beans. Various forms

parmesan cheese

are available, from soft silken tofu to a firm type which can be cubed and sautéed. Tempeh is similar to tofu, but has a nuttier taste. Keep filo pastry, shortcrust and puff pastry in the freezer, but allow plenty of time for slow thawing. Nuts will also store well in the freezer.

tofu

sour cream and crème fraîche

From the Larder

If your store cupboard (pantry) is well stocked, spur-of-the-moment meals will never be a problem. In addition to pasta, pulses and grains, dry goods should include different types of flour, easy-blend (rapid-rise) dried yeast, polenta and oatmeal, and you'll also want a small supply of nuts. Don't buy these in bulk, as nuts become rancid if stored for too long. Dried mushrooms are useful, as are sun-dried tomatoes and (bell) peppers, but you may prefer to buy the ones that come packed in oil in jars. Also in jars, look for pesto (both green and red), tahini,

mixed nuts

canned beans

peanut butter, capers and olives. Useful sauces include passata (bottled strained tomatoes), creamed horseradish, soy sauce, black bean sauce and the vegetarian versions of oyster sauce and Worcestershire sauce. You'll need various vinegars, including balsamic and rice vinegar, and oils, especially olive, sunflower, sesame, and groundnut (peanut) oil. For low-fat cooking, a light oil spray is useful.

Cans take up quite a lot of space, but it is well worth keeping a stock of favourites, such as canned tomatoes, kidney beans, borlotti beans, flageolets or cannellini and chickpeas, plus corn kernels, artichoke hearts and bamboo shoots. Canned coconut milk comes in handy for vegetable curries and some soups.

wine vinegar

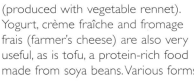

Techniques

Even the simplest tasks in the kitchen can take longer than necessary if you don't know a few useful techniques and short cuts. Below are some step-by-step instructions for preparing a variety of ingredients that will save time and help to make vegetarian cooking easier. No special equipment is required for most of them, just a sharp knife.

Chopping Herbs

1 Remove any thick stalks and discard. Chop the herbs finely, in both directions, using a sharp knife or a mezzaluna – half-moon herb chopper – which you use in a see-saw motion.

Preparing Chillies

1 Wearing rubber gloves if possible, halve the chilli lengthways. Leave the seeds inside or scrape out and discard.

2 Slice or chop the chilli finely. Wash the knife, board and your hands, if not gloved, in hot soapy water, as chillies can burn sensitive skin. Never rub your eyes or touch your lips after handling chillies.

Peeling & Chopping Tomatoes

1 Cut a cross in the blossom end of each tomato. Put them in a heatproof bowl and pour over boiling water.

2 Leave for 30 seconds, until the skins wrinkle and start to peel back from the crosses. Drain, peel off the skin and chop the flesh neatly.

Crushing Garlic

1 Break off a clove of garlic and smash it firmly with the flat side of a wide knife blade. Pick off the skin. Chop the clove, sprinkle over a little table salt, then use the flat side of the knife to work the salt into the garlic until reduced to a paste.

Preparing Fresh Root Ginger

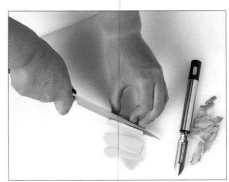

1 Peel the skin off a piece of fresh root ginger. Cut the ginger in thin slices. Then cut each slice into thin strips and use, or turn the strips around and chop them finely. Ginger can also be grated, in which case it need not be peeled.

Preparing Pulses

1 Rinse well, pick out any small stones, then put the pulses in a bowl with plenty of cold water. Soak for 4–8 hours.

2 Drain the pulses, rinse them under cold water and drain them again. Tip them into a pan. Add plenty of cold water but no salt. Bring to the boil, boil hard for 10 minutes, then simmer until tender. Drain and season.

> **Cook's Tip**
> *Lentils do not need to be soaked. Red lentils become very soft when cooked and are ideal for purées. Green or brown lentils are firmer and retain more texture. The finest flavoured are Puy lentils.*

Basic Recipes

The recipes in this book are largely complete in themselves, but there are a few basics that crop up again and again, such as tomato sauce and mayonnaise. You can substitute bought versions, but do make your own if you have time.

Vegetable Stock
Makes about 2.4 litres/4 pints/10 cups
2 large onions, coarsely chopped
2 leeks, sliced
3 garlic cloves, crushed
3 carrots, coarsely chopped
4 celery sticks, sliced
a large strip of pared lemon rind
12 fresh parsley stalks
a few fresh thyme sprigs
2 bay leaves
2.4 litres/4 pints/10 cups water

1 Put the chopped vegetables in a large pan. Add the lemon rind, with the parsley, thyme and bay leaves. Pour in the water and bring to the boil. Skim off the foam that rises to the surface.

2 Lower the heat and simmer, uncovered, for 30 minutes. Strain, season it to taste and leave it to cool. Cover and keep in the refrigerator for up to 5 days, or freeze for up to 1 month.

Cook's Tip
To save freezer space, boil vegetable stock down to concentrate it to about half the original quantity and then freeze in ice cube trays. When thawing add an equal amount of water.

French Dressing
Makes about 120ml/4fl oz/ ½ cup
90ml/6 tbsp olive oil
15ml/1 tbsp white wine vinegar
5ml/1 tsp French mustard
pinch of granulated sugar
salt and ground black pepper

1 Place the oil and vinegar in a screw-top jar. Add the mustard and sugar. Close the lid and shake. Season to taste.

Mayonnaise
Makes about 350ml/12fl oz/1 ½ cups
2 egg yolks
15ml/1 tbsp Dijon mustard
30ml/2 tbsp lemon juice or white wine vinegar
300ml/ ½ pint/1 ¼ cups oil (vegetable, corn or light olive)
salt and ground black pepper

1 Put the egg yolks, mustard, half the lemon juice or vinegar and a pinch of salt in a blender or food processor and process for 10 seconds to mix. With the motor running, add the oil through the funnel in the lid, drop by drop at first and then in a steady stream, processing constantly until the mayonnaise is thick and creamy. Taste and sharpen with the remaining juice or vinegar, if you like, and season to taste.

Tomato Sauce
Makes about 350ml/12fl oz/1 ½ cups
15ml/1 tbsp olive oil
1 onion, finely chopped
1 garlic clove, crushed
400g/14oz can chopped tomatoes
15ml/1 tbsp tomato purée (paste)
15ml/1 tbsp chopped fresh mixed herbs (parsley, thyme, oregano, basil)
pinch of granulated sugar
salt and ground black pepper

1 Heat the oil in a pan and cook the onion and garlic gently until softened. Stir in the tomatoes, tomato purée, herbs and sugar, with salt and pepper to taste.

2 Simmer, uncovered, for 15–20 minutes, stirring occasionally, until the mixture has reduced and is thick. Use immediately or cool, cover and store in the refrigerator.

Cook's Tip
Use this tomato sauce on pizzas or pasta. It also tastes excellent with vegetables. Spoon it over cooked cauliflower, top with grated cheese and grill (broil) until bubbly.

Index